Addison-Wesley

Algebra

Enrichment

Created for use with *Addison-Wesley Algebra* Student Text

Stanley A. Smith
Randall I. Charles
John A. Dossey
Mervin L. Keedy
Marvin L. Bittinger

▲▼ Addison-W   ny

Menlo Park, California · Reading,   ·k
Don Mills, Ont   ..., England
Amsterdam · Bonn · Sydney · Singapore · Tokyo
Madrid · San Juan

ISBN 0-201-25352-6

7 8 9 10 - AL - 95 94 93

Contents

Bonus Topic Worksheets

The following 15 blackline masters are self-contained enrichment worksheets designed for above-average students.

Using each worksheet, students will learn about a "higher" mathematical topic, either historical, abstract, or theoretical in nature. Topics include measuring the rational numbers on the number line, Fermat's Little Theorem, and LaGrange's method for finding the roots of polynomials.

These extension topics are fully presented on each worksheet. Challenging exercises either follow the exposition or are fully integrated within the text of the worksheet. These worksheets would be ideal to give to your best students while the rest of your class spends extra time reviewing more difficult concepts in the text. Good students should require little or no help from the teacher and should be able to complete each worksheet in 20 to 40 minutes.

Binary Operations

A binary operation is a way to "operate" on two members of a set in order to produce a member of the same set. Addition, for example, is a binary operation on the set of whole numbers. If you operate by adding two whole numbers, you will always produce a whole number. Division is not a binary operation on the set of whole numbers because division of two whole numbers does not always produce a whole number. For example, $21 \div 4 = 5\frac{1}{4}$.

EXERCISES

Tell whether the operation is binary on the given set.

1. division on the non-zero fractions

2. multiplication on the whole numbers

3. addition on the odd whole numbers

4. multiplication on the whole numbers divisible by 3

5. multiplication on the whole numbers divisible by 23

Commutativity and Associativity

A binary operation $*$ is commutative on a given set if for every two members a and b of the set, $a * b = b * a$.

A binary operation $*$ is associative on a given set if for every two members a and b of the set, $a * (b * c) = (a * b) * c$.

EXERCISES

Suppose $a * b$ is a binary operation that means "multiply a by itself b times."

6. Find $2 * 5$.   7. Find $3 * 4$.   8. Find $\frac{2}{5} * 3$.

9. Give an example to show that $*$ is not associative on the set of whole numbers.

Suppose $a \not\! c \, b$ is a binary operation that means "choose a, the first number."

10. Find $8 \not\! c \, 2$.   11. Find $2 \not\! c \, 8$.   12. Is $\not\! c$ commutative on the set of integers?

The table at the right shows the results of applying the binary operation # to a, b, and c.

#	a	b	c
a	b	a	c
b	a	c	b
c	c	b	a

13. Is # commutative on the set (a, b, c)?

14. Is # associative?

Use of the binary operation § gives the following results:

$$7 \,\S\, \frac{2}{3} = 49 \qquad \frac{2}{3} \,\S\, 7 = \frac{4}{9} \qquad 10 \,\S\, 3 = 100 \qquad 12 \,\S\, 10 = 144$$

15. Find $5 \,\S\, 4$.   16. Find $5 \,\S\, 2$.   17. Find $A \,\S\, B$.

2   *Algebra Enrichment*

Modular Arithmetic

Addition of numbers on the face of a clock can produce sums that are different from those obtained by normal addition. Seven hours after 10 o'clock, it is 5 o'clock. So, in "clock arithmetic," $10 + 7 = 5$. Only the whole numbers from 1 to 12 are used as answers in clock arithmetic. A number larger than 12 can be reduced to a clock number by subtracting from it the largest multiple of 12 that is smaller than the number itself. For example, the number 40 can be reduced to a clock number by subtracting 3×12, or 36, from it. So, 40 is equivalent to 4.

Clock arithmetic is an example of a **modular system.** To indicate that 40 is equivalent to 4 in the system utilizing only the whole numbers from 1 to 12, we write $40 = 4$ (mod 12). The modular 9 system uses only the whole numbers from 1 to 9. To find 7×3 (mod 9), you multiply normally; then you subtract from the product the largest multiple of 9 that is less than the product.

$$7 \times 3 = 21$$
$$21 - 2(9) = 21 - 18 = 3$$
$$\text{So, } 7 \times 3 \text{ (mod 9)} = 3$$

EXERCISES

Evaluate each expression.

1. $8 + 5$ (mod 12)

2. 1×6 (mod 6)

3. 7×7 (mod 9)

4. 14×2 (mod 16)

5. $10 - 2$ (mod 13)

6. $4 \times 3 \times 2$ (mod 5)

7. 5×4 (mod 10)

8. 3^4 (mod 4)

9. 8×8 (mod 8)

10. Complete this multiplication table for the mod 4 system.

	1	2	3	4
1	1	2	3	4
2	2	4	2	4
3				
4				

Use the results above to solve these equations.

11. $2m = 4$ (mod 4)

12. $4k = 4$ (mod 4)

Solve for x.

13. $x + 3 = 1$ (mod 4)

14. $x + 8 = 3$ (mod 12)

15. $3x = 3$ (mod 6)

Find m.

16. $4 \times 2 = 3$ (mod m)

17. $4 \times 6 = 4$ (mod m)

18. $5 \times 11 = 7$ (mod m)

19. Find $p + p$ (mod p).

20. Find $p \times p$ (mod p).

21. Find $(p - 1) + (p - 1)$ (mod p).

How Many Parakeets?

To find the number of parakeets you will need the following clues.

1. Sam's shoe size is one-quarter the number of minutes it took Li Hua to wash her sheepdog.

2. The number of players on the Lizard City tiddlywinks team is 7 more than the number of rutabaga plants in Carlos's window box.

3. Talasi's golf score was 1 less than 3 times the number of parakeets in the Lizard City Zoo.

4. The number of sour notes that Marie hit while playing "Ramona" on her sousaphone was 6 less than 6 times the number of avocados that Max used in his guacamole.

5. If Talasi's golf score is increased by 10, the result is 3 times the number of minutes it took Li Hua to wash her sheepdog.

6. The number of players on the Lizard City tiddlywinks team is 1 less than 4 times the number of avocados that Max used in his guacamole.

7. The number of rutabaga plants in Carlos's window box is 5 less than twice Sam's shoe size.

QUESTION: If Marie hit 24 sour notes while playing "Ramona" on her sousaphone, then how many parakeets are there in the Lizard City Zoo?

To solve, follow these steps:

1. Use clue #4 to find the number of avocados that Max used in his guacamole.

2. Use clue #6 and your answer to the preceding question to find how many players there are on the Lizard City tiddlywinks team.

3. Use clue #2 and your answer to the preceding question to find how many rutabaga plants there are in Carlos's window box.

4. Use clue #7 and your answer to the preceding question to find Sam's shoe size.

5. Use clue #1 and your answer to the preceding question to find how long it took Li Hua to wash her sheepdog.

6. Use clue #5 and your answer to the preceding question to learn Talasi's golf score.

7. Use clue #3 and your answer to the preceding question to find how many parakeets there are in the Lizard City Zoo.

Equivalence Relations

In Chapter 2 you studied the reflexive, symmetric, and transitive properties of equality.

Reflexive Property	**Symmetric Property**	**Transitive Property**
$a = a$ is always true.	If $a = b$, then $b = a$.	If $a = b$ and $b = c$, then $a = c$.

Are there similar properties for inequalities? Consider the "is less than" relationship. If the reflexive property is to hold, then $a < a$ must always be true. Since a clearly is not less than itself, there is no reflexive property for "is less than."

Similarly, there is no symmetric property because if $a < b$, then b cannot be less than a. However, the transitive property holds because if $a < b$ and $b < c$, then $a < c$.

A relation that is reflexive, symmetric, and transitive is called an **equivalence relation.** "Equality," or $=$, is an equivalence relation because equality is reflexive, symmetric, and transitive. "Is less than," or $<$, is not an equivalence relation because even though the transitive property holds, the reflexive and the symmetric properties do not.

EXERCISES

For each of the following relations, tell whether it is (a) reflexive, (b) symmetric, (c) transitive, and (d) an equivalence relation.

1. "is greater than or equal to" ($\geq$)
2. "is not equal to" ($\neq$)
3. "is married to"
4. "was born on the same day as"
5. "is a brother of"
6. "has the same zip code as"
7. "is perpendicular to"
8. "is as tall as"
9. "is parallel to"
10. "is a sibling of"
11. "rides the same bus as"
12. "is in the same algebra class as"

Expanding Binomials

Consider the following expanded powers of the binomial $x + y$.

$(x + y)^0 = 1$
$(x + y)^1 = x + y$
$(x + y)^2 = x^2 + 2xy + y^2$
$(x + y)^3 = x^3 + 3x^2y + 3xy^2 + y^3$
$(x + y)^4 = x^4 + 4x^3y + 6x^2y^2 + 4xy^3 + y^4$

Look for patterns in the expansions. Find as many patterns as you can. Then observe the following.

1. The first term is always x raised to the same power to which the binomial on the left is raised.
2. After the first term, the exponent of x decreases by one each term.
3. The first appearance of y occurs in the second term where it is raised to the first power.
4. Thereafter, the exponent of y increases by one each term.

Now you can determine the exponents of x and y in each term of the expansion for any power of $(x + y)$.

To find the correct coefficients, you can use *Pascal's Triangle,* named after the seventeenth-century mathematician Blaise Pascal.

Row 1   1
Row 2   1   1
Row 3   1   2   1
Row 4   1   3   3   1
Row 5   1   4   6   4   1
Row 6   1   5   10   10   5   1

Each number in the triangle is obtained by adding the two numbers directly above. The coefficients for the expansion of $(x + y)^n$ are the numbers found in Row $n + 1$. For example, the coefficients for $(x + y)^5$ are found in Row 6. Thus,

$(x + y)^5 = x^5 + 5x^4y + 10x^3y^2 + 10x^2y^3 + 5xy^4 + y^5$

EXERCISES

Expand.

1. $(x + y)^6$ **2.** $(m + n)^7$ **3.** $(a + b)^8$

Expand and simplify.

4. $(p + 2)^3$ **5.** $(c^2 + 3)^4$

6. Find the last term in the expansion of $(72 + m)^{21}$.

7. Find the second term in the expansion of $(a^3 + 5)^{11}$.

8. Find the next-to-last term in the expansion of $(6 + p)^7$.

NAME _____

DATE _____

Euclid's Algorithm

Removing the common factor is probably the most frequently used method of factoring.

   EXAMPLE $15x + 20 = 5(3x + 4)$

Common-factor factoring is easy when you can quickly spot the common factor, like the 5 in the example above. But suppose you want to factor $272x + 935$. If there is a common factor, it certainly isn't obvious. *Euclid's Algorithm* helps you to find not just a common numerical factor, but the greatest common factor. The algorithm is named after Euclid of Alexandria, the Greek mathematician who codified the principles of plane geometry in his text *The Elements* more than 2000 years ago.

   EXAMPLE   Factor $272x + 935$.

First, express the larger of the two coefficients as the greatest multiple possible of the smaller coefficient, plus the remainder.	$935 = 3 \times 272 + 119$
Repeat this step for 272 and 119.	$272 = 2 \times 119 + 34$
Repeat again for 119 and 34.	$119 = 3 \times 34 + 17$
Continue the procedure until you obtain a remainder of 0.	$34 = 2 \times 17 + 0$
The greatest common factor of the original expression is 17, the next-to-last remainder.	$272x + 935 = 17(16x + 55)$

EXERCISES

Factor.

1. $323x + 133$

2. $600m + 420$

3. $273x + 63$

4. $141p - 893$

5. $1071s + 867$

6. $273w - 299$

7. $1183x - 490$

8. $452a + 565$

Who Stole the Cheesecake?

A bus left Origin at 4:00 p.m. on a nonstop run to Abscissa 30 miles north. It arrived at 4:45 p.m., waited 15 minutes, and then returned to Origin at the same rate. The driver remembered seeing a cheesecake on Mrs. Quadrant's windowsill, 24 miles from Origin, on the way north, but she was certain that it was gone when she passed on the return run.

In their efforts to solve the cheesecake crime, the police uncovered the following facts:

1. Tom, Dora, Harry, and Joan all live on the Origin-Abscissa Road.

2. Tom left his house 17 miles from Origin at 3:30 p.m. and walked 9 miles north to Curley's Gas Station, arriving at 5:45 p.m.

3. Dora left her house 12 miles from Origin at 3:15 p.m. and rode her bicycle north at 9 miles per hour to Abscissa.

4. Harry left his house 2 miles north of Origin at 3:00 p.m., drove north for one-half hour at 40 miles per hour, stopped at the Polynomial Museum for 45 minutes, and then drove to Curley's Gas Station, arriving simultaneously with Tom.

5. Joan left her house 20 miles north of Origin at 5:00 p.m. and jogged to Curley's, arriving simultaneously with Tom and Harry.

Use the graph to plot the travels of Tom, Dora, Harry, Joan, and the Origin-Abscissa bus. (The first two parts of the bus trip have been graphed to get you started.) Assume that everyone traveled at a constant rate of speed.

Analyze your results to discover who stole Mrs. Quadrant's cheesecake.

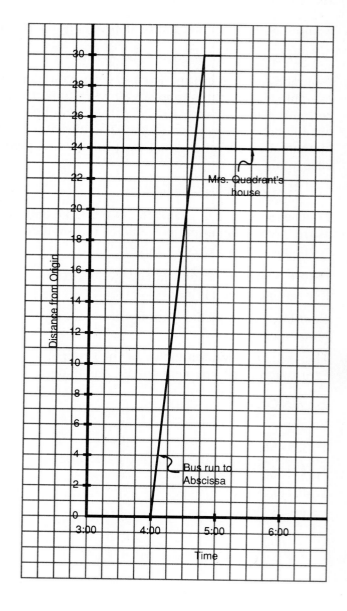

Diophantine Analysis

An equation in two variables may have an infinite number of solutions. But if the stipulation is made that the solutions must be integers, then the number of solutions may be greatly reduced or even eliminated. For example, $x^2 + y^2 = 25$ has an infinite number of solutions. However, of the solutions, only $(3, 4)$, $(3, -4)$, $(-3, 4)$, and $(-3, -4)$ are integers. There also are an infinite number of solutions for $x^2 - y^2 = 2$, but none of them are integers.

Diophantine analysis is used to find the integral solutions, if they exist, to an equation. Diophantus, a Greek mathematician who lived during the third century B.C., was the first to study this class of problems. Diophantine analysis can be an extremely complex process. However, a relatively simple approach works well for first-degree equations since it involves only algebra and inspired guesswork.

EXAMPLE   Find an integral solution to $3x - 7y = 14$.

First, isolate on the left side the term with the smaller coefficient.

$$3x = 7y + 14$$

Express the terms on the right side as the largest possible multiples of the left-side coefficient, plus remainder.

$$3x = 6y + y + 12 + 2$$

Rearrange, placing remainders together.

$$3x = 6y + 12 + y + 2$$

Divide both sides of the equation by the left-side coefficient.

$$x = 2y + 4 + \frac{y + 2}{3}$$

Look at the fraction on the right side.

Choose an integral value for the variable that will make the fraction an integer.

$$y = 1 \rightarrow \frac{y + 2}{3} = \frac{1 + 2}{3} = 1$$

Substitute the chosen value of the variable in the original equation to find the value of the second variable.

$$3x - 7(1) = 14$$
$$3x = 14 + 7$$
$$3x = 21$$
$$x = 7$$

$(7, 1)$ is an integral solution to $3x - 7y = 14$.

EXERCISES

Find an integral solution to each.

1. $-10a + 7b = -23$

2. $6x - 5y = 21$

3. $7x + 11y = 358$

4. $17m - 35n = 46$

5. Diane and Dusty purchased some 22¢ stamps and some 14¢ stamps, spending $1.34 altogether. How many of each type did they buy?

Lattice Points

Nokonyu owns two more pistachio trees than Julio owns. If you let x equal the number of trees that Julio owns and y equal the number of trees that Nokonyu owns, then $y = x + 2$.

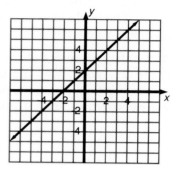

Figure 1

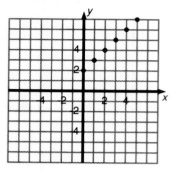

Figure 2

The graph of the equation $y = x + 2$ is shown in Figure 1 above. Although this graph is meaningful in a mathematical sense, most of it is not meaningful as a representation of the relationship between the numbers of trees owned by Nokonyu and Julio. In the real world, there are neither negative pistachio trees nor fractions of pistachio trees. Thus, a more appropriate graph would show only those points with whole numbers as the x and y coordinates, as is shown in Figure 2 above. A point is called a **lattice point** if both its x and y coordinates are integers.

EXERCISES

1. Amalita purchased four more rose bushes than Aretha purchased. Draw a graph showing the relationship between the numbers of rose bushes that the two purchased.

2. Elaine owned two more than three times as many elm trees as Elmer owned. Draw a graph showing the relationship between the numbers of elm trees the two owned.

3. There were two spruce trees in front of Lincoln High School and at least one spruce tree in front of Washington Junior High School. Draw a graph showing the relationship between the numbers of spruce trees at the two schools.

4. Find all lattice points that satisfy both $2 < x < 5$ and $-3 < y < 1$.

5. Find all lattice points that satisfy both $-10 \leq x < -7$ and $7 \leq y < 9$.

6. Find all lattice points that satisfy the equation $x^2 + y^2 \leq 5$.

10   *Algebra Enrichment*

Continued Fractions

The fraction shown at the right is a **continued fraction.** Instead of the simple denominator found in most fractions, the denominator of a continued fraction consists of a whole number (5 in the example) plus a second fraction with 1 as the numerator. The

$$\cfrac{1}{5 + \cfrac{1}{3 + \cfrac{1}{2 + \frac{1}{4}}}}$$

denominator of the second fraction likewise consists of a whole number plus another fraction. Each fraction in the continuing series has the same form: a 1 as the numerator and a sum as the denominator.

To simplify a continued fraction, start at the bottom right and work upwards one step at a time.

$$\cfrac{1}{5 + \cfrac{1}{3 + \cfrac{1}{2 + \frac{1}{4}}}} = \cfrac{1}{5 + \cfrac{1}{3 + \cfrac{1}{\frac{9}{4}}}} = \cfrac{1}{5 + \cfrac{1}{3 + \frac{4}{9}}} = \cfrac{1}{5 + \cfrac{1}{\frac{31}{9}}} = \cfrac{1}{5 + \frac{9}{31}} = \cfrac{1}{\frac{164}{31}} = \frac{31}{164}$$

Every fraction can be changed into a continued fraction.

EXAMPLE Change $\frac{67}{350}$ into a continued fraction.

First, divide the denominator by the numerator, expressing the quotient as a whole number plus remainder. Continue dividing, using the pattern shown in Step 1 below, until you obtain a remainder of 0.

Second, take the quotients in order, disregarding the remainders. The resulting sequence (5,4,2,7) gives the whole-number portions of the continued fraction, as shown in Step 2 below.

Step 1

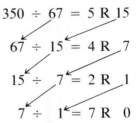

$$350 \div 67 = 5 \text{ R } 15$$
$$67 \div 15 = 4 \text{ R } 7$$
$$15 \div 7 = 2 \text{ R } 1$$
$$7 \div 1 = 7 \text{ R } 0$$

Step 2

$$\frac{67}{350} = \cfrac{1}{5 + \cfrac{1}{4 + \cfrac{1}{2 + \frac{1}{7}}}}$$

EXERCISES

Simplify.

1. $\cfrac{1}{3 + \frac{1}{2}}$

2. $\cfrac{1}{8 + \cfrac{1}{5 + \frac{1}{3}}}$

3. $\cfrac{1}{6 + \cfrac{1}{5 + \cfrac{1}{4 + \frac{1}{3}}}}$

4. $\cfrac{1}{2 + \cfrac{1}{2 + \cfrac{1}{2 + \frac{1}{2}}}}$

Express each fraction as a continued fraction.

5. $\frac{31}{222}$

6. $\frac{11}{112}$

7. $\frac{68}{157}$

8. $\frac{109}{360}$

Algebra Enrichment 11

Pythagorean Triples

The Pythagorean theorem states that for every right triangle with legs of lengths a and b and hypotenuse of length c, the following is true.

$$a^2 + b^2 = c^2$$

If a, b and c are integers, then the three numbers a, b, and c are called a **Pythagorean triple.** For example, the numbers 3, 4, and 5 are a Pythagorean triple because $3^2 + 4^2 = 9 + 16 = 25 = 5^2$.

An easy way to find Pythagorean triples is to substitute integral values of n in the three expressions $2n + 1$, $2n^2 + 2n$, and $2n^2 + 2n + 1$. For example, if $n = 2$, then the resulting values are 5, 12, and 13. These numbers are a Pythagorean triple because $5^2 + 12^2 = 25 + 144 = 169 = 13^2$.

EXERCISES

1. Let $n = 4$, and find the resulting Pythagorean triple.

2. Let $n = 6$, and find the resulting Pythagorean triple.

One disadvantage of the system described above is that it generates only certain Pythagorean triples. To find *all* Pythagorean triples, you can use the following procedure.

Let $a = p^2 - q^2$, $b = 2pq$, and $c = p^2 + q^2$.

Choose values of p and q that satisfy the following conditions.

1. Both are positive whole numbers where $p > q$.
2. One number is odd; the other number is even.
3. p and q do not share a common factor.

For example, if $p = 2$ and $q = 1$, then $a = 3$, $b = 4$, and $c = 5$. As seen above, the numbers 3, 4, and 5 are a Pythagorean triple.

EXERCISES

3. Complete a chart like the one below for all pairs (p, q) where $p = 2, 3, 4, 5, 6,$ and 7.

		a	b	c
p	q	$p^2 - q^2$	$2pq$	$p^2 + q^2$
2	1	3	4	5
3	2			

4. Look at your completed chart. Is it true that either a or b is always divisible by 3? What is true about their divisibility by 4?

5. What can you say about the values of a, b and c regarding their divisibility by 5?

6. What can you say about the values of a, b, $a + b$, and $a - b$ regarding their divisibility by 7?

Function Variation

Radius	Circumference	Surface area	Volume
r	$2\pi r$	$4\pi r^2$	$\frac{4}{3}\pi r^3$

Radius		Circumference		Surface area		Volume	
1		2π		4π		$\frac{4}{3}\pi$	
times 3		times 3		times 9		times 27	
3		6π		36π		36π	
times 3		times 3		times 9		times 27	
9		18π		324π		972π	
times 3		times 3		times 9		times 27	
27		54π		2916π		$26{,}244\pi$	

The chart above shows the relationships among the radius, circumference, surface area, and volume of a sphere when the radius is multiplied by 3.

1. The circumference, which varies directly as the radius, is multiplied by 3.
2. The surface area, which varies directly as the square of the radius, is multiplied by 3^2.
3. The volume, which varies directly as the cube of the radius, is multiplied by 3^3.

This pattern leads to the following generalizations.

If y varies directly as x raised to the nth power, then multiplication of x by a constant c will result in y multiplied by c^n.

$$y = kx^n$$
$$(c^n)y = k(cx)^n$$

If y varies inversely as x raised to the nth power, then multiplication of x by a constant c will result in y divided by c^n.

$$y = \frac{k}{x^n}$$
$$\frac{y}{c^n} = \frac{k}{(cx)^n}$$

EXERCISES

1. The distance an object falls varies directly as the square of the time it falls. How many times farther does an object fall in 6 seconds than it does in 2 seconds?

2. The intensity of light striking you varies inversely as the square of the distance between you and the source. Compare the intensity of a candle 40 ft away with that of a similar candle 8 ft away.

3. The cost of krypton varies directly as the cube of the weight and inversely as the age. The gem Krypton K is three times the weight and five times the age of Krypton P. If Krypton P sells for $5 million, then what is the cost of Krypton K?

4. The number of eucalyptus leaves that a koala bear eats in a day varies directly as the fourth power of the bear's height, directly as its age, and inversely as the square of the height of the bear's nest above the ground. Ko-ko Koala is 1 ft tall, 12 years old, and nests 50 ft above the ground. Her Uncle Koo-koo is 2 ft tall, 18 years old, and nests 100 ft above the ground. If Ko-ko eats 1000 leaves per day, how many leaves does Uncle Koo-koo eat?

Parabolic Orbits

Comets travel through the solar system in orbits that are approximately parabolic. As they approach the sun, they are drawn in by the gravitational pull of the sun, coming nearest the sun at the vertex of their orbits. Then they swing around and speed off in the opposite direction into the depths of the solar system.

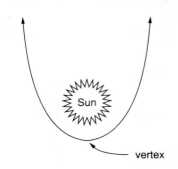

vertex

If a comet is observed at three different points in its orbit, then an equation that describes the orbit can be found.

EXAMPLE   A comet has been observed at points (2,9), (1,4), and $(-1,0)$. Find the parabolic equation of its orbit.

Since a parabola is the graph of a quadratic equation, each ordered pair must satisfy the general quadratic equation $y = ax^2 + bx + c$. When you substitute the coordinates of the given points, you get these equations.

$\boxed{1}$ $9 = 4a + 2b + c$ $\boxed{2}$ $4 = a + b + c$ $\boxed{3}$ $0 = a - b + c$

The system can be solved by addition and substitution.

$4 = a + b + c$ Equation $\boxed{2}$ $9 = 4a + 2b + c$ Equation $\boxed{1}$

$0 = a - b + c$ Equation $\boxed{3}$ $0 = 2a - 2b + 2c$ Doubling Equation $\boxed{3}$

$4 = 2a + 2c$ Sum $9 = 6a + 3c$

$a = 2 - c$ Solve for a

Substitute $\longrightarrow 9 = 6(2 - c) + 3c$

$9 = 12 - 6c + 3c$

$3c = 3$

$c = 1$

By substitution you find that $a = 1$ and $b = 2$. Therefore, the equation of this comet's orbit is $y = x^2 + 2x + 1$.

EXERCISES

Each exercise gives three points on the orbit of a comet.

Find the equation of the orbit.

1. $(1,3), (-1,1), (2,7)$ **2.** $(0,-1), (1,-1), (2,3)$

3. $(1,0), (0,-4), (2,6)$ **4.** $(0,-5), (1,-1), (-1,-1)$

The Law of Sines

Given an angle and the length of a side of a right triangle, you can use trigonometric functions to determine the lengths of other sides of the triangle. Suppose, however, that the triangle is not a right triangle.

EXAMPLE $A = 28°$, $C = 42°$, and $c = 12$ cm. Find a.

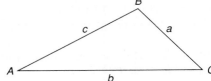

Because the sine, cosine, and tangent functions are defined only for right triangles, you must construct some right triangles in the figure. Do this by constructing $\overline{BD}$ perpendicular to $\overline{AC}$.

$$\sin 28° = \frac{BD}{12} \qquad \sin 42° = \frac{BD}{a}$$

$$12 \sin 28° = BD \qquad a \sin 42° = BD$$

Since BD is equal to both $12 \sin 28°$ and $a \sin 42°$, you can write:

$$12 \sin 28° = a \sin 42°$$

$$a = \frac{12 \sin 28°}{\sin 42°}$$

$$a \approx \frac{12(0.4695)}{0.6691} \approx 8.42 \text{ cm}$$

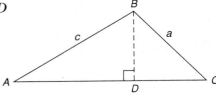

You can generalize this procedure. Given any triangle ABC, construct BD perpendicular to AC. Then the following is true.

$$\sin A = \frac{x}{c} \qquad \sin C = \frac{x}{a}$$

$$c \sin A = x \qquad a \sin C = x$$

Therefore, $c \sin A = a \sin C$,

and $\dfrac{a}{\sin A} = \dfrac{c}{\sin C}$.

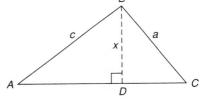

By similar reasoning, you can show these both equal to $\dfrac{b}{\sin B}$.

This important relationship is called the Law of Sines.

EXERCISES

Find the length a in each triangle.

1.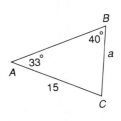

2.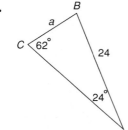

3.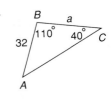

4.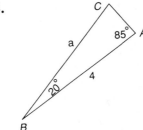

Probability in Heredity

The basic laws of heredity were discovered during the nineteenth century by the Austrian monk and botanist Gregor Mendel. Mendel found that traits in humans and plants are controlled by pairs of units located in cells. We now call these units *genes*. A *pure trait* consists of two identical genes. A *hybrid trait* consists of two different genes. A trait is *dominant* if it dominates other genes, preventing them from showing up in offspring. Otherwise, the trait is *recessive*.

EXAMPLE 1   A pure dominant yellow pea plant is crossed with a pure recessive green pea plant. What are the possible outcomes?

By labeling dominant genes with capital letters and recessive genes with lower-case letters, a heredity chart can be constructed. All four possible offspring are Yg. Since Y dominates g, all are yellow. Since the genes are different, all offspring are hybrids.

	g	g
Y	Yg	Yg
Y	Yg	Yg

EXAMPLE 2   Two Yg offspring are now crossed. What are the possible outcomes?

Three of the four possible offspring are yellow. One is green. Since all four possibilities are equally likely, there is one chance in four that the offspring will be green. So, the probability that the offspring will be green is $\frac{1}{4}$.

	Y	g
Y	YY	Yg
g	Yg	gg

EXERCISES

1. A dominant yellow pea plant Yg is crossed with a pure recessive green pea plant. What is the probability that the offspring will be green?

2. Brown eyes are dominant over blue eyes in humans. If a man with Bb brown eyes marries a woman with blue eyes, what is the probability
   a. that their first child will have blue eyes?
   b. that their first child will have brown eyes?

3. A man with blue eyes marries a woman with blue eyes. What is the probability that their first child will have brown eyes?

4. Tall pea plants are dominant over short ones. What is the probability that a tall yellow plant $TsYg$ and a short yellow plant $ssYg$ will produce a short green plant when crossed?

Critical Thinking Worksheets

The following 15 blackline masters are self-contained enrichment worksheets that vary in level of difficulty.

Using each worksheet, students will learn critical-thinking skills, such as examining assumptions, making plausible inferences, distinguishing relevant from irrelevant facts, supplying evidence for a conclusion, recognizing contradictions, and refining generalizations.

Students will learn how to avoid oversimplification, how to look at ideas from different perspectives, how to clarify ideas, how to raise questions, and how to generate or assess solutions. Learning these skills will help foster independent thinking, one goal of critical thinking.

Before you try to solve the match puzzles, review these assumptions.

There are 14 squares in the drawing below.

There are 3 squares in the drawing below.

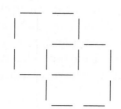

The drawing below shows crisscrossed matches. They are allowed only if specified in the problem.

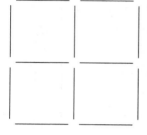

Solve the following match puzzles.

1. **a.** Take away 2 matches to make 2 squares of different sizes.
   b. Move 3 matches to make 3 congruent squares.
   c. Move 4 matches to make 3 congruent squares.
   d. Move 2 matches to form 7 squares, not all the same size. (You can crisscross matches.)
   e. Move 4 matches to make 10 squares, not all the same size. (You can crisscross matches.)

2. Take away 4 matches to make 4 equilateral triangles, all the same size.

3. Move 4 matches to make 3 squares, not all the same size.

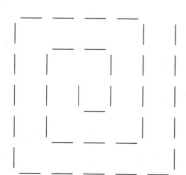

Directions: Each question or group of questions is based on a given set of conditions. To answer some of the questions it may be useful to make a table or draw a diagram. Select the best answer from the choices given.

Craig is a sales representative who must visit major clients in various cities. On his trip he must see clients in at least three of these four cities: Louisville, Memphis, Nashville, and Omaha. His trip must be planned according to the following restrictions.

1. He can visit a city only once during the trip.
2. He cannot visit both Louisville and Nashville.
3. His first visit must be to Louisville or Omaha.
4. His last visit must be to Memphis or Omaha.
5. He must visit Memphis before Nashville if he visits both cities.

1. Which of the following travel plans, each of which lists cities in the order in which Craig would visit them, conforms to the restrictions?

   A. Louisville, Nashville, Omaha

   B. Omaha, Louisville, Memphis, Omaha

   C. Omaha, Louisville, Memphis

   D. Nashville, Omaha, Memphis

   E. Omaha, Memphis, Nashville

2. Which of the following plans, each of which lists cities in the order in which Craig would visit them, does *not* conform to the restrictions?

      Plan 1: Louisville, Omaha, Memphis
      Plan 2: Omaha, Nashville, Louisville, Memphis
      Plan 3: Omaha, Louisville, Memphis

   A. Plan 1 only

   B. Plan 2 only

   C. Plans 1 and 2 only

   D. Plans 1 and 3 only

   E. Plans 2 and 3 only

3. If Craig visits Omaha last, he must visit

   A. Memphis last.

   B. Nashville before Louisville.

   C. Louisville before Nashville.

   D. Louisville first.

   E. all four cities.

4. If Craig visits Omaha second, he must visit

   A. Louisville first.

   B. Memphis last.

   C. exactly three cities.

   D. Omaha before Memphis.

   E. all of the above.

5. Craig's trip cannot include which of the following plans?

   A. a visit to exactly 3 cities

   B. a visit to Omaha before Louisville

   C. a visit to Louisville before Omaha

   D. a visit to Memphis

   E. a visit to Nashville

NAME _____

DATE _____

Directions: Each question or group of questions is based on a given set of conditions. To answer some of the questions it may be useful to make a table or draw a diagram. Select the best answer from the choices given.

Ayame, Bianca, Cleon, Doug, and Eula are making presentations at a conference on urban planning. Two will make their presentations before lunch. Immediately after lunch, two short films will be shown. Then the final three presentations will be made.

Doug refuses to be either the first or the last person to make a presentation. Eula must make her presentation immediately after Ayame completes her presentation. Cleon has to leave the conference at lunchtime to fly back to her home office.

1. Which of the following represents a possible schedule for the conference?

   A. Cleon, Bianca, lunch, films, Ayame, Eula, Doug

   B. Ayame, Eula, Cleon, lunch, films, Doug, Bianca

   C. Cleon, Ayame, lunch, films, Eula, Doug, Bianca

   D. Bianca, Cleon, lunch, films, Doug, Ayame, Eula

   E. Cleon, Ayame, Eula, lunch, Doug, films

2. If Bianca must be first, then how many possible different orderings of the presentations are possible?

   A. 0   **B.** 1   **C.** 2   **D.** 3   **E.** 4

3. Who *must* make a presentation in the morning?

   A. Ayame   **B.** Bianca   **C.** Cleon   **D.** Doug   **E.** Eula

4. Which of the following is a complete and accurate list of those who could not be first?

   A. Ayame only   **B.** Doug only

   C. Ayame or Doug only   **D.** Ayame, Doug, or Eula only

   E. Ayame, Cleon, or Doug only

5. Which of the following is a complete and accurate list of those who could make the final presentation?

   A. Ayame only   **B.** Ayame or Bianca only

   C. Doug or Cleon only   **D.** Bianca or Eula only

   E. Bianca, Eula, or Ayame only

6. If Cleon makes the first presentation, then which of the following is a list in the correct order of presentation of those who could make their presentations after lunch?

      List 1: Eula, Doug, Bianca
      List 2: Ayame, Eula, Bianca
      List 3: Doug, Ayame, Eula

   A. List 2 only   **B.** Lists 1 and 2 only

   C. Lists 2 and 3 only   **D.** Lists 1 and 3 only

   E. All three lists

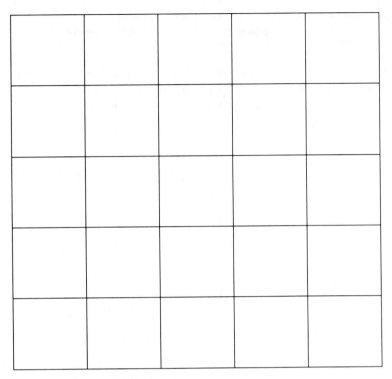

Shown above is a picture of a large quilt. Your job is to make two smaller quilts out of this large one. The quilts must both be square. You must cut the large quilt into four pieces that can then be put together to make the two smaller quilts.

Consider these questions before you begin.

- How many squares are there in the large quilt?
- Can the smaller quilts each be the same size? Why or why not?
- How can you use graph paper to help you plan where to cut?
- If you are having difficulty, first try to form two smaller quilts by making more than four pieces.
- If you want a hint, then look below.

Hint: Two of the pieces are made up of squares 4, 5, 9, and 10 and squares 13, 14, 15, 20, and 25.

1	2	3	4	5
6	7	8	9	10
11	12	13	14	15
16	17	18	19	20
21	22	23	24	25

Directions: Each question or group of questions is based on a given set of conditions. To answer some of the questions it may be useful to make a table or draw a diagram. Select the best answer from the choices given.

Joe, Jill, Jane, and Jim are all drivers going for a ride in the same car. Joe gets nervous when Jill or Jim drives. Jim gets nervous when he or Jane drives. Jane gets nervous when Joe or Jim drives, and Jill gets nervous when anyone drives other than herself.

1. Which driver would make the greatest number of people nervous?

   A. Joe **B.** Jill **C.** Jane **D.** Jim

   E. Joe and Jane equally **F.** Jim and Jill equally

2. Which driver would make the least number of people nervous?

   A. Joe **B.** Jill **C.** Jane **D.** Jim

   E. Jill and Jane equally **F.** Joe and Jim equally

3. Who should drive if Jim is not to be nervous?

   A. Joe **B.** Jill **C.** Jane **D.** Jim

   E. Either Joe or Jill **F.** Either Jane or Jim

4. Who should drive if neither Jane nor Joe is to be nervous?

   A. Joe **B.** Jill **C.** Jane **D.** Jim

   E. Either Jane or Joe **F.** Either Jim or Jill

5. Jill has too much homework to do, and she decides not to go for the ride. Now, which driver would make the least number of people nervous?

   A. Joe **B.** Jill **C.** Jane **D.** Jim

   E. Joe and Jane equally **F.** Jim and Jane equally

6. Joy decides to go in place of Jill. Joy gets nervous only when Joe drives, and Jane gets nervous when Joy drives. Now, which driver would make the least number of people nervous?

   A. Joe **B.** Joy **C.** Jane **D.** Jim

   E. Joe and Joy equally **F.** Joy and Jane equally

NAME _____

DATE _____

Directions: Each question or group of questions is based on a given set of conditions. To answer some of the questions it may be useful to make a table or draw a diagram. Select the best answer from the choices given.

Francine is a representative of a major consulting firm. The firm she works for has a client in each of these five cities: Austin, Baltimore, Charlotte, Dallas, and Evansville. Francine is planning a business trip to visit at least three of these cities subject to the following conditions.

  1. She must visit Austin or Evansville first.
  2. She must visit Charlotte or Evansville last.
  3. If she visits Austin, then she also must visit Dallas.
  4. She cannot visit both Baltimore and Charlotte.

1. Which of the following travel plans, each of which lists the cities in the order that Francine would visit them, does *not* conform to the restrictions.

   A. Austin, Dallas, Evansville

   B. Evansville, Dallas, Charlotte

   C. Austin, Baltimore, Dallas, Evansville

   D. Austin, Baltimore, Dallas, Charlotte

   E. Evansville, Dallas, Austin, Charlotte

2. If Francine visits Evansville first, then which of the following facts must also be true?

   Fact 1: She does not visit Baltimore.
   Fact 2: She visits Dallas.
   Fact 3: She visits Charlotte last.

   A. Fact 1 only   **B.** Fact 3 only

   C. Facts 1 and 2 only   **D.** Facts 1 and 3 only

   E. Facts 1, 2, and 3

3. If Francine visits Evansville last, then which of the following facts must also be true?

   Fact 1: She visits Baltimore.
   Fact 2: She does not visit Charlotte.
   Fact 3: She visits Dallas.

   A. Fact 1 only   **B.** Fact 2 only

   C. Fact 3 only   **D.** Facts 1 and 2 only

   E. Facts 2 and 3 only

4. Which of the following must Francine's itinerary include?

   A. visits to exactly three cities

   B. visits to exactly four cities

   C. a visit to Dallas

   D. a visit to Baltimore

   E. a visit to Charlotte

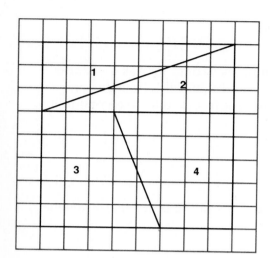

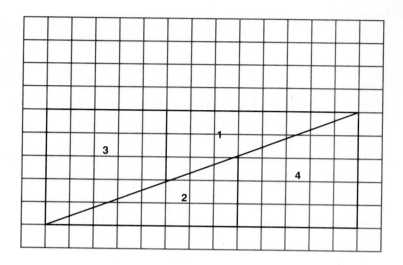

Joel has a square piece of material that is 8 units long on each side. He wants to cut it apart to make a rectangular-shaped mat that is 13 units long and 5 units wide. He made the two drawings shown above to illustrate how he plans to cut apart the square to make the mat.

Joel's twin sister, Janice, looks at the two drawings and observes that the dimensions of the square are 8 units by 8 units, which means that it has an area of 64 square units; the dimensions of the rectangle are 5 units by 13 units, which means that it has an area of 65 square units. "You are a magician," she tells Joel. "You have created another square unit out of thin air." Did Joel really do this?

The drawing at the right shows the diagonal on Joel's sketch with points labeled *A, B,* and *C* and another segment drawn from *B* perpendicular to the side of the rectangle.

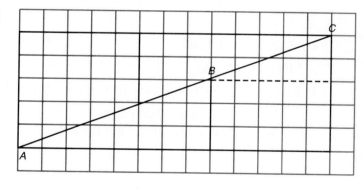

1. What is the slope (rise over run) of segment *AC*?

2. What is the slope of segment *AB*?

3. What is the slope of segment *BC*?

4. Compare the results. Where is the square unit that Joel "created out of thin air?"

If you have a problem finding the extra square unit, then try this: On a piece of graph paper, mark off a square with each side 8 units long. Cut it apart as shown in the first drawing at the top of the page. Then try to fit the pieces together as shown in the other drawing at the top of the page.

Directions: Each question or group of questions is based on a given set of conditions. To answer some of the questions it may be useful to make a table or draw a diagram. Select the best answer from the choices given.

An air traffic controller must make quick decisions that involve lives. The job requires getting all planes in safely and on time with as few adjustments to planned schedules as possible. Suppose you are an air traffic controller at a small airport that has four runways and various types of aircraft that can be classified as follows.

    Type A aircraft can land on runways 1 or 2.
    Type B aircraft can land on runway 3 only.
    Type C aircraft can land on runways 1, 2, or 4.
    Type D aircraft can land on runways 2 or 3.

1. A type A, a type B, and a type C aircraft all wish to land at the same time. Which is the most appropriate schedule for the landings?

    A. A on 1; B on 3; C on 2

    B. A on 2; B on 3; C on 4

    C. A on 1; B on 3; C on 2 or 4

    D. A on 1 or 2; B on 3; C on 1, 2, or 4, but not the same runway as A

2. Two type C, one type A, and one type D all wish to land at the same time. Which is the most appropriate schedule for the landings?

    A. A on 1; D on 3; C on 2 and 4

    B. A on 2; D on 3; C on 4

    C. A on 1; D on 2 or 3; C on 2 and 4

    D. A on 1 or 2; D on 2 or 3; C on 1, 2, or 4, but not the same runway as A

3. Two type A, one type B, one type C, and one type D all wish to land immediately. Which is the most appropriate schedule for the landings?

    A. A on 1 and 2; B on 3; C on 4; D on 2

    B. A on 2; B on 3; C on 4; D on 1

    C. A on 1 and 2; B on 3; C on 2 or 4; D on 3

    D. A on 1 and 2; B on 3; C on 4; D scheduled later on 2 or 3

4. A type A has radioed for an emergency landing. Already scheduled are a type B on runway 3, a type C on runway 1, and a type D on runway 2. Which is the best readjustment to the schedule?

    A. A on 2; B on 3; C on 4; D scheduled later on 2

    B. A on 1; B on 3; C on 4; D on 2

    C. A on 1; B on 3; C on 2; D on 4

    D. A on 1; B on 3; C on 2; D scheduled later on 2

5. Runway 2 must be closed immediately for snow removal. Already scheduled are a type A on runway 1, a type C on runway 2, and a type D on runway 3. Which is the best readjustment to the schedule?

    A. A on 1; D on 3; C scheduled later on 1   **B.** A on 2; C on 1; D on 3

    C. A on 1; C on 4; D on 2   **D.** A on 1; C on 4; D on 3

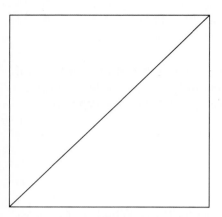

Figure 1

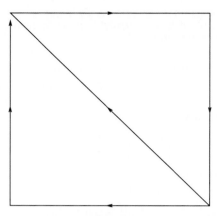

Figure 2

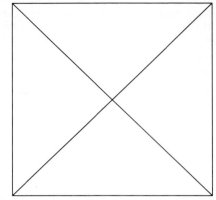

Figure 3

To draw unicursally means to draw without lifting the pencil from the paper or going over a line more than once. Figure 1 can be drawn unicursally, as shown in Figure 2. Figure 3 cannot be drawn unicursally.

Draw the following figures unicursally.

1.

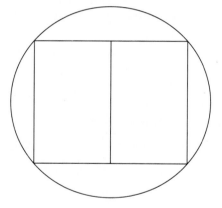

2.

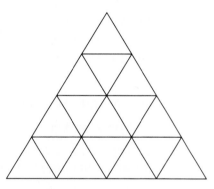

3.

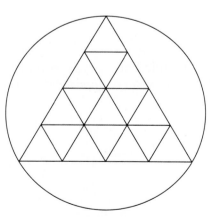

4.

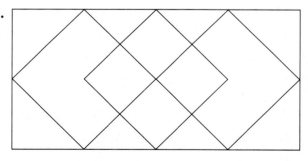

CRITICAL THINKING 10
For use with Chapter 10

An archaeologist found some ancient writings in arithmetic that were decipherable. The archaeologist studied the writings and learned that:

 represents 22 objects.

 represents 300,102 objects.

 represents 111,000 objects.

Use the archaeologist's discovery to tell the number represented by each of the following writings.

1.

2.

3.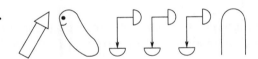

4.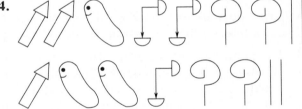

5.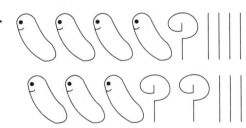

6.

Suppose you were the ancient writer. How would you show each number?

7. 30

8. 42

9. 401

10. 2002

11. 30,001

12. 111,111

Algebra Enrichment 27

At Belmont High School, courses in English, mathematics, social studies, and science are required. Two additional electives must be chosen.

Erica wants auto shop and a foreign language as electives. Rosario wants at least one class with Erica and Lani together. Rosario wants music and psychology as electives. Lani wants home economics and art as electives.

The following tells the periods of the school day during which each course is conducted.

English is offered 1st or 2nd period.
Mathematics is offered 1st, 5th, or 6th period.
Social studies is offered 3rd or 5th period.
Science is offered 3rd or 4th period.
Auto shop is offered 5th or 6th period.
Music is offered 1st period.
Home economics is offered 3rd period.
Spanish and German are offered 2nd period.
Psychology is offered 4th period.
Art is offered 2nd or 3rd period.

1. Write a schedule that will accommodate Erica, Rosario, and Lani.

2. Erica decides that she will take mathematics first period and art third period. Rosario decides that she wants to take art instead of psychology. Can a new schedule be worked out to accommodate everyone's wishes? If so, write the schedule.

3. Erica decides to transfer from art back into a foreign language. Can she keep her mathematics class first without upsetting Rosario? Write a schedule that resolves all of Erica's problems.

4. The school decides not to offer German this year, and Erica has already studied Spanish. What are Erica's choices for second period without rearranging her schedule? With rearrangement of her schedule, what are Erica's choices if she still wants auto shop but does not care if her schedule matches those of her friends?

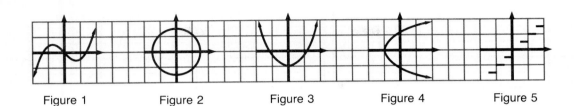

Figure 1   Figure 2   Figure 3   Figure 4   Figure 5

1. Some of the five figures shown above are graphs of functions and some are not. Which of the following statements is true?

   A. Figures 1 and 3 are the only graphs of functions.

   B. Figures 1, 3, 4, and 5 are the only graphs of functions.

   C. Figures 1, 3, and 5 are the only graphs of functions.

   D. Figures 3 and 5 are the only graphs of functions.

2. Which of the following is a true statement about graphs of functions?

   A. No y value has more than one x value.   **B.** No x value has more than one y value.

   C. All x values have more than one y value.   **D.** All y values have more than one x value.

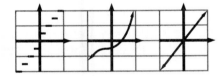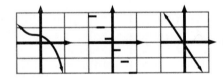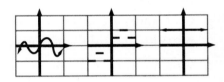

These graphs of functions are increasing.

These graphs of functions are decreasing.

These graphs of functions are neither increasing nor decreasing.

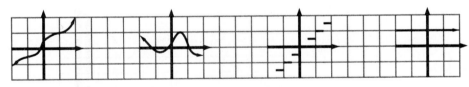

Figure 6   Figure 7   Figure 8   Figure 9

3. Which statement is true about the graphs of functions shown above?

   A. Figures 6 and 8 are increasing; 7 is decreasing; 9 is neither.

   B. Figures 6 and 8 are increasing; 7 is increasing; 9 is neither.

   C. Figures 6 and 8 are increasing; 7 and 9 are neither increasing nor decreasing.

   D. Figure 6 is increasing; 7 and 9 are decreasing; 8 is neither.

4. Which statement is true about graphs of increasing functions?

   A. They are going up to the left forever.

   B. They are going up to the right forever.

   C. They alternate going up and down forever.

   D. Both statements A and B are true.

Algebra Enrichment   29

These graphs have a
maximum value.

These graphs have a
minimum value.

These graphs have no
maximum or minimum.

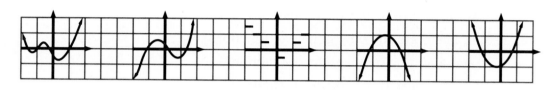

Figure 1   Figure 2   Figure 3   Figure 4   Figure 5

1. Which statement is true about the graphs in Figures 1–5 shown above?

   A. They all have maximum or minimum values.

   B. Figures 1, 3, and 5 have minimum values; 4 has a maximum value.

   C. Figures 1 and 4 have maximum values; 3 has a minimum value.

   D. Only figures 1 and 3 have minimum values.

2. Which is a true statement about maximum or minimum values on graphs?

   A. All graphs have either a maximum or a minimum value.

   B. If a graph has a maximum value, then it also has a minimum value.

   C. A graph that has a maximum value looks like a valley.

   D. A graph that has a maximum value looks like a mountain.

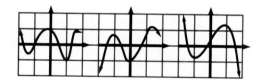

These graphs have local maximum and
minimum values.

These graphs do not have a local maximum or
minimum value.

3. Which statement is true about local maximum or minimum values?

   A. A graph with a local maximum cannot have a local minimum value.

   B. A local minimum value is the lowest point on the graph in a region of points around the minimum point.

   C. A local maximum value is the lowest point on the graph in a region of points around the minimum point.

   D. A graph with a local minimum cannot have a local maximum value.

Directions: Each question or group of questions is based on a given set of conditions. To answer some of the questions it may be useful to make a table or draw a diagram. Select the best answer from the choices given.

A stable has 100 horses that it rents to equestrians. Of these horses, 15 are for beginners only, 23 are for beginners and intermediates, 20 are for intermediates only, 25 are for intermediates and advanced, and 17 are for advanced only. On one extremely busy weekend, 32 beginners, 30 intermediates, and 18 advanced equestrians reserve horses. The manager starts with this list of possibilities.

  15   beginner-only horses to beginners
  17   beginner-intermediate horses to beginners
  16   intermediate-only horses to intermediates
   6   beginner-intermediate horses to intermediates
   8   intermediate-advanced horses to intermediates
   1   intermediate-advanced horse to advanced
  17   advanced-only horses to advanced

1. Select the modification of the manager's list that is *not* possible.

    A. Change 6 to 5 and 8 to 9.

    B. Change 16 to 20, 6 to 0, and 8 to 10.

    C. Change 16 to 18, 6 to 0, and 8 to 12.

    D. Change 16 to 14, 6 to 14, and 8 to 2.

2. Tell which of the following modifications leaves the most available horses for each level of beginners, intermediate, or advanced riders who might walk in to rent a horse.

    A. Change 16 to 20, 6 to 5, and 8 to 5.

    B. Change 16 to 20, 6 to 0, and 8 to 10.

    C. Change 16 to 18 and 6 to 4.

    D. Change 6 to 0 and 8 to 14.

3. A group of 20 additional advanced equestrians calls to ask if it can reserve horses. Which modification is the best considering this new development?

    A. Change 16 to 20 and 8 to 4.

    B. Change 6 to 14 and 8 to 0.

    C. Change 16 to 18 and 8 to 6.

    D. Change 16 to 10 and 8 to 14.

4. After the 20 additional advanced equestrians show up in Problem 3, another group of 15 intermediate equestrians wants to know whether horses can be available for them. Answer the question and tell which explanation helps you to answer.

    A. Yes, there are more than 15 horses left for intermediates.

    B. No, there are only 4 horses left for intermediates only.

    C. Yes, there are exactly 15 horses left for intermediates.

    D. No, there are no horses left for intermediates.

Directions: Each question or group of questions is based on a given set of conditions. To answer some of the questions it may be useful to make a table or draw a diagram to help you find the answer.

There are 6 index cards lying face down on a table as shown above. Exactly two of these cards have the number 3 written on the hidden side, and you do not know which cards they are. You pick two cards at random.

1. What is the probability that you will pick at least one 3?

2. What is the probability that you will not pick a 3?

3. Are you more likely to pick a 3 or to not pick a 3?

The six faces on a number cube have the numbers from 1 to 6 shown on them. If you roll one number cube, your chances of rolling the number 5 are 1 in 6, or $\frac{1}{6}$. If you roll two number cubes, your chances of rolling a 5 increase. You would think that your chances would be $\frac{1}{6}$ for each number cube, or $\frac{1}{6} + \frac{1}{6}$ or $\frac{1}{3}$ when you roll two. The more number cubes   that you roll, the better your chances become. For example, you might think that when you roll six number cubes, your chances of rolling a 5 are $\frac{1}{6} \times 6$, or 1. But a probability of 1 means that you would always roll a 5 when you roll six number cubes. You should know that this is not true. What went wrong?

4. Look over the assumptions that were made to find one or more that were wrong. Then show how or why it or they were wrong.

Manipulative Activity Worksheets

The following 15 blackline masters contain manipulative activities designed to heighten students' understanding of algebra by having them construct physical models of algebraic concepts. Each activity is appropriate for all levels of students.

Using each worksheet, students are led through a step-by-step process of constructing a manipulative model. Then they use the model to solve algebraic exercises. Through this process, students gain new insights and a more concrete understanding of how and why many abstract concepts work.

These sheets are appropriate to be assigned independently as homework or to be completed in class in small groups. To construct the manipulatives, students will often need access to scissors, construction paper, colored pencils, rulers, etc. The box at the top of each worksheet clearly indicates the materials needed for the activity.

As a final note, manipulatives are not new to mathematics. Great discoveries in mathematics and science had their basis in physical objects and phenomena. (Recall the story of Isaac Newton and the apple.) Also, manipulatives are commonly used in elementary and junior high school classrooms and are not unfamiliar to students. Manipulative activities at this level, therefore, will continue to deepen and enhance the students' understanding of mathematical concepts and skills.

Turns and Flips

Draw an arrow on one side of a square-shaped piece of paper. Then flip over the paper and draw an arrow on the other side. Make sure that both arrows point the same way. Then explore the following operations.

■ *You will need:*

■ *square piece of paper*

R	**L**	**V**	**H**
right turn	left turn	vertical flip	horizontal flip
$\left(\frac{1}{4}\text{ turn clockwise}\right)$	$\left(\frac{1}{4}\text{ turn counter-clockwise}\right)$	$\left(\frac{1}{2}\text{ rotation around the vertical axis}\right)$	$\left(\frac{1}{2}\text{ rotation around the horizontal axis}\right)$

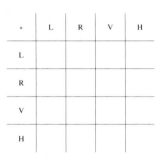

start   stop   start   stop   start   stop   start   stop

1. Complete the table by showing the results for each pair of turns or flips. The * means "followed by." Do the turn or flip on the left side of the table first, followed by the turn or flip shown at the top of the table. Always have the arrow pointing up before you begin each time.

*	L	R	V	H
L				
R				
V				
H				

2. Explore the commutative property for pairs of turns and flips. Draw an arrow to show each result. Remember that * means "followed by." A letter preceded by the number 2 means to do the turn or flip twice.

   a. R * L _____   **b.** L * R _____   **c.** H * V _____   **d.** V * H _____

   e. R * H _____   **f.** H * R _____   **g.** 2L * V _____   **h.** V * 2L _____

3. Is the operation * commutative? (Can you change the order of the turns and flips without affecting the results?)

4. Explore the associative property. Do the part in parentheses first.

   a. (R * L) * R _____   **b.** R * (L * R) _____   **c.** (R * L) * V _____

   d. R * (L * V) _____   **e.** (2R * V) * H _____   **f.** 2R * (V * H) _____

5. Is the operation * associative?

MANIPULATIVE ACTIVITY 2

For use with Lesson 2-1

NAME _____

DATE _____

Binary Punch Cards

Binary numbers consist of the digits 0 and 1 only. Each place has a value two times the value of the place to the right. In this activity, you will make cards to represent binary numbers.

Cut off one corner and punch four holes through an index card. Label the holes as shown. Use this card as a pattern to cut and punch the other 15 cards.

Number the cards from 0 to 15. Then cut slots to show the binary number for each base ten number. Slots represent 1's; no slots represent 0's.

■ *You will need:*

■ *16 index cards or art paper, scissors, paper punch, a paper clip or pencil*
■

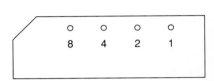

EXAMPLES:

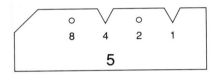

$$0(8) + 1(4) + 0(2) + 1(1)$$
$$= 0101_{\text{base two}}$$
$$= 5_{\text{base ten}}$$

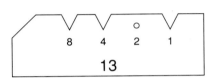

$$1(8) + 1(4) + 0(2) + 1(1)$$
$$= 1101_{\text{base two}}$$
$$= 13_{\text{base ten}}$$

Before you begin the exercises below, shuffle the cards. At the completion of each exercise, shuffle them again. Always make sure that the diagonal corners are together after each shuffle.

1. Without looking at the faces of the cards, locate the card for the binary number 1011 by using the following method:
   First, put a straightened paper clip or a pencil through all the holes in the 8's place. Since there is a 1 in the 8's place in 1011, discard the cards that stay on the clip. Next, put the clip in the 4's place. Keep those cards that stay on the clip, since there is a 0 in the 4's place in 1011. Continue with the 2's place and the 1's place.

   a. Did you keep those cards that stayed on the clip when it was inserted in the 2's place? Why or why not?

   b. Did you discard those cards that fell off the clip when it was inserted in the 1's place? Why or why not?

   c. You should have one card left. Turn it over. What is the base ten number for 1011?

2. Locate the cards for the following binary numbers using the method outlined in Exercise 1. Then write the base ten number for each.

   a. 0010   **b.** 0110   **c.** 1110

3. How would you find the cards for base ten numbers less than 8?

4. How would you find the cards for base ten numbers that are odd?

Balanced Equations

You can make a balance scale. Drill a hole in the center of a meter stick or ruler. Relabel the markings on the stick so that the numbering begins at the hole and proceeds outward to each edge.

Hammer into a block of wood an unheaded nail smaller than the hole that you drilled in the meter stick. Wrap a rubber band around the nail about 1 cm below the top of the nail. Put the nail through the hole.

Set the scale on a level surface. Check for balance. If necessary, weight the higher side with rubber bands until the stick is level.

Use counters for weights. Show each of the following on the scale. Solve for x.

■ *You will need:*

■ *balance scale or hammer, nail, counters, meter stick, block of wood, and rubber bands.*
■ _____

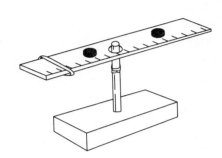

1. $4x = 12$ On the right side, put a counter on 12. On the left side, stack 4 counters where they balance 12.

   $x =$ _____

2. $10 + 3x = 8 \cdot 2$ Put a counter on 10 on the left side and 2 counters on 8 on the right side. Stack 3 counters on the left side to make the scale balance.

   $x =$ _____

3. $3x + 6 = 5 \cdot 3$ Put a counter on 6 on the left side and 3 counters on 5 on the right side. Stack 3 counters on the left side to make the scale balance.

   $x =$ _____

4. $9 < x + 2$ Put a counter on 9 on the left side and a counter on 2 on the right side. Move a counter along the right side until the scale begins to tip to the right.

   $x >$ _____

Continue to use the balance scale to solve for x.

5. $6x = 3x + 9$

   $x =$ _____

6. $4x < 5 + 7$

   $x <$ _____

7. $4x + 7 > (6 \cdot 3) + 1$

   $x >$ _____

8. $6x + 1 = 5 \cdot 5$

   $x =$ _____

9. $5 + 4x = 3x + 7$

   $x =$ _____

10. $4x - 4 > 8 + 2x$

   $x >$ _____

Calder Mobiles

Mobiles are moving, three-dimensional, abstract sculptures. Many consist of flat shapes suspended from rods on wire and balanced so perfectly that they move freely and gracefully in the air. This art form was invented about 1930 by Alexander Calder, who used his extensive mathematics background in the construction of these sculptures.

You can use your knowledge of equations to create your own mobiles. Cut identical shapes from cardboard and punch a hole at the top center of each shape. Use string to suspend the shapes from straws the distances shown in the drawings at the right. Use the number of shapes indicated. An oblong shape with the number 3 on it, for example, requires the use of 3 shapes, which would make it weigh 3 times as much as a shape with the number 1 on it.

You will need:

- cardboard, scissors, string or fishing nylon, plastic straws, ruler, and hole punch

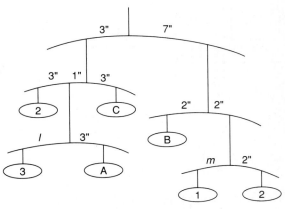

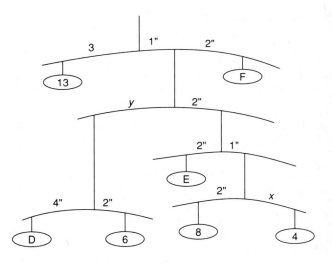

Mobile A

1. Make Mobile A. Determine how many shapes you will need at *A*, *B*, and *C* through experimentation. Do the same to find the lengths at *l* and *m*.

   $A =$ _____ $l =$ _____

   $B =$ _____ $m =$ _____

   $C =$ _____

2. Using what you have discovered about balancing mobile structures, find the values of *D*, *E*, *F*, *x*, and *y* for Mobile B.

   $D =$ _____ $x =$ _____

   $E =$ _____ $y =$ _____

   $F =$ _____

3. Design and make your own mobile. Use the oblong shapes that you already have or design your own shapes. Draw a diagram of your mobile. Include information about distances and weights on your diagram.

Mobile B

Five Square

You can use base-ten blocks to show the squares of numbers. To show 15^2, for example, make a square with each side 15 units long. In this activity, you will examine squares of numbers that have a 5 in the ones place.

■ *You will need:*

■ *base-ten blocks or graph paper cut into 10 × 10 squares, 10 × 1 rectangles, and 1 × 1 squares*

EXAMPLE 1 $15^2 = 225$

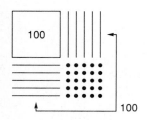

EXAMPLE 2 $25^2 = 625$

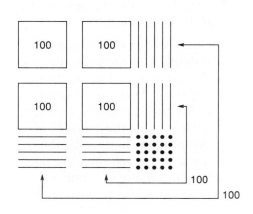

Now use your base-ten blocks to find these squares.

1. 35^2 **2.** 45^2 **3.** 55^2 **4.** 65^2

Look for a pattern in the blocks.

5. How many unit blocks are there in each square number?

6. How many hundreds blocks are there in each square number?

7. Fill in the blanks at the right. Then describe the pattern.

$15^2 =$ _____ hundreds + 25

$25^2 =$ _____ hundreds + 25

$35^2 =$ _____ hundreds + 25

$45^2 =$ _____ hundreds + 25

$55^2 =$ _____ hundreds + 25

$65^2 =$ _____ hundreds + 25

8. If x represents the number of tens in a number, then the number of hundreds in the square of the number can be represented by the product of x and what expression?

Use the pattern to find these squares.

9. 75^2 **10.** 85^2 **11.** 95^2

12. If x represents the value of the digit in the tens place, then which of the following statements, if any, are true?

A. $(10x + 5)^2 = (10x + 5)(10x + 5)$

B. $(10x + 5)^2 = 100x^2 + 100x + 25$

C. $(10x + 5)^2 = 100x(x + 1) + 25$

MANIPULATIVE ACTIVITY 6
For use with Lesson 6-4

NAME _____

DATE _____

Modeling Polynomials

You can make algebra tiles this way: Cut out some $2'' \times 2''$ squares, some $\frac{3''}{8} \times \frac{3''}{8}$ squares, and some $2'' \times \frac{3''}{8}$ rectangles from cardboard. Color one side of each piece.

■ *You will need:*

■ *algebra tiles or cardboard, ruler, and scissors*
■

Think of the small square as representing the integer 1, and the rectangle as representing x. Then the large square represents x^2. The colored sides represent negative numbers.

You can use the tiles to model and factor polynomials.

EXAMPLE 1	EXAMPLE 2	EXAMPLE 3
Polynomials:		
$x^2 + 5x + 6$	$x^2 - 8x + 7$	$x^2 - 2x - 15$

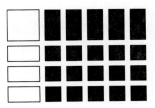

Factors:		
$(x + 3)(x + 2)$	$(x - 7)(x - 1)$	$(x - 5)(x + 3)$

Write the polynomial and the factors represented by each set of tiles.

1.   **2.**   **3.**

   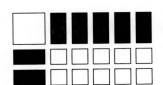   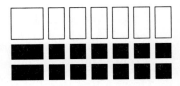

Use your tiles to model each polynomial. Draw your model and write the related factors.

4. $x^2 + 8x + 15$ **5.** $x^2 - 6x + 9$ **6.** $x^2 + 7x + 12$

7. $x^2 - 8x + 15$ **8.** $x^2 - 11x + 10$ **9.** $x^2 + 9x + 8$

10. $x^2 + 2x - 15$ **11.** $x^2 - 7x - 18$ **12.** $x^2 - 6x - 16$

Data Fitting

Foot-length is measured from the end of the heel to the tip of the big toe. Forearm-length is measured from the elbow to the wrist. Do you think that a predictable relationship exists between these two measurements in people of all ages?

Measure the foot-length and forearm-length of at least 25 people of different ages. Consider each pair of measurements as an ordered pair and plot them on a graph such as the one at the right.

The graph you are making is a **scattergram**. If the points on a scattergram cluster around a line, then a relationship, or **correlation**, between the two measurements may exist.

■ *You will need:*

■ *centimeter ruler, graph paper, and pencil*

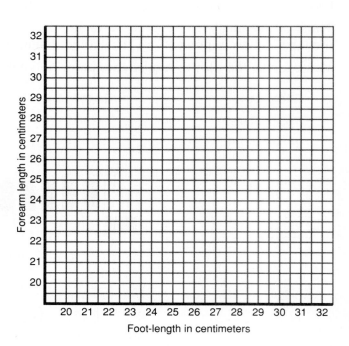

1. Complete your scattergram. Does it show that a correlation may exist?

2. A *positive correlation* exists when one factor increases as the other factor increases. A *negative correlation* exists when one factor increases as the other decreases. Does your graph show a positive or a negative correlation? If so, which?

3. Draw a line on your graph so that there are as many data points above the line as below. Let *x* represent foot-length and *y* represent forearm-length. Write an equation for the line.

4. Draw a line parallel to the first line so that all the data points are on this line or below it. Write the equation of the new line.

5. Draw another line parallel to the first so that all the data points are on the line or above it. Write the equation of the new line.

6. Predict the forearm-length for each foot-length. Use the equation from Exercise 3 to find the best estimate. Use the equations from Exercises 4 and 5 to find a range of least and greatest estimates.

Foot-Length	Forearm-Length		
	Best estimate	Least estimate	Greatest estimate
23 cm			
27 cm			
25.5 cm			

MANIPULATIVE ACTIVITY 8

For use with Lesson 8-1

NAME _____

DATE _____

Graphing to Decode

Letters are associated with points on this
graph. They will be used as you decode the
secret word.

■ *You will need:*

■ *pencil and ruler*

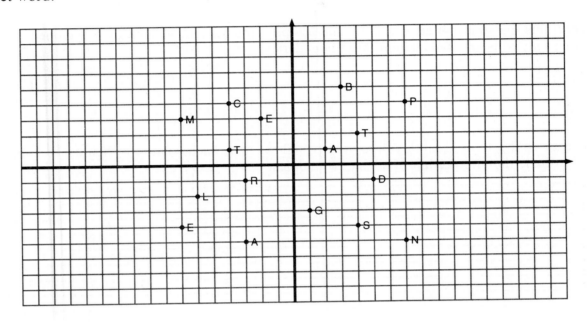

To decode the secret word, solve each system of equations graphically. Draw the lines on the
graph shown above. If the solution corresponds to a point associated with a letter, then write the
letter in the appropriate blank below.

1. $x + y = 3$
$x - y = 1$

2. $x = 3y$
$3y - 6 = 2x$

3. $x = \frac{1}{3}y + 2$
$-2x - y = 1$

4. $3x - 3y = -15$
$-3x - 3y = -3$

5. $x + y = 8$
$-x + 2y = 7$

6. $x - 3y = 0$
$5x - y = -14$

7. $-x - y = 8$
$2x - y = -1$

The secret word that you will write below comes from an Arabic word that means the reuniting
of broken parts. It was first used by an Arabic mathematician around 825 A.D.

_____ _____ _____ _____ _____ _____ _____
   1   2   3   4   5   6   7

Size Limitations

The U.S. Postal Service enforces certain
restrictions on the size of the mail that it will
deliver. These restrictions can be described by
a system of linear inequalities.

■ *You will need:*

■ *pencil, ruler, and graph paper*

If l represents the length of an envelope, and h represents the height, then the envelope is
permitted only if its size falls within these boundaries:

$$l \leq 11\frac{1}{2}''$$

$$h \leq 6\frac{1}{8}''$$

$$\frac{l}{h} \leq 2\frac{1}{2}$$

$$l \geq 5''$$

$$h \geq 3\frac{1}{2}''$$

$$\frac{l}{h} \geq 1\frac{1}{3}$$

Graph each of the six inequalities. Use your pencil to shade each solution. Then use a colored
pencil to shade the intersection of all six inequalities.

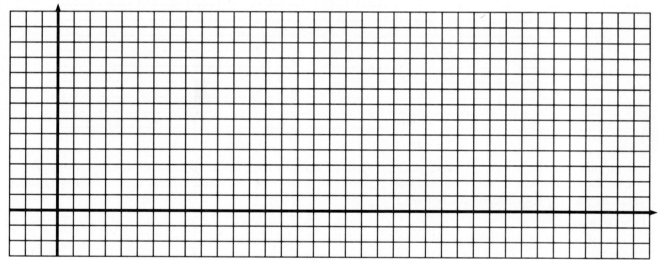

Use your graph to check the following sizes of envelopes.

Will they pass the Postal Service's restrictions?

1. $6'' \times 3''$

2. $5\frac{1}{4}'' \times 4''$

3. $11'' \times 4''$

4. $9'' \times 6''$

5. $7\frac{3}{4}'' \times 5''$

6. $10\frac{3}{4}'' \times 4\frac{3}{4}''$

Make a template.

Make an actual-size template that shows the acceptable size ranges of envelopes. Use a large
sheet of one-inch graph paper. Draw the x and y axes and then shade the area of the paper that
you have colored above. Use the template for checking envelopes this way: Align the lower left
corner of an envelope with the intersection of the x and y axes. If the upper right corner is in the
shaded area, then the letter is acceptable.

Dividing Polynomials

You can make and use algebra tiles like those shown below to model dividing with polynomials.

■ *You will need:*

■ *algebra tiles or cardboard, ruler, and scissors*

x^2 $-x^2$ x $-x$ 1 -1

EXAMPLE 1: $\dfrac{x^2 + 4x + 4}{x + 2} = x + 2$

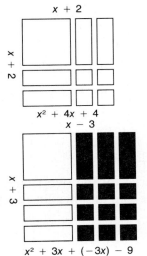

$x + 2$

$x^2 + 4x + 4$

Arrange the tiles in a rectangular shape so that one side represents the divisor and the whole shape represents the dividend. Then the other side will show the quotient.

EXAMPLE 2: $\dfrac{x^2 - 9}{x + 3} = x - 3$

$x - 3$

$x^2 + 3x + (-3x) - 9$

Tiles representing both positive and negative expressions must be used. To show the quotient, you will use a white block for x^2 and 9 black unit tiles for -9. To undo the adding of 3 white x-tiles for the divisor, you must add 3 black x-tiles when showing the dividend.

EXAMPLE 3: $\dfrac{x^2 + 2x - 12}{x - 3} = x + 5 + \dfrac{3}{x - 3}$

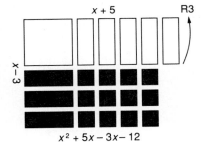

$x + 5$ R3

$x^2 + 5x - 3x - 12$

If there are too many or too few single tiles to form a rectangle, then write the quotient plus or minus the remainder over the divisor.

Use your tiles to model each of the following. Draw the models on a separate sheet of paper and write the quotient.

1. $\dfrac{x^2 + 5x + 6}{x + 2}$

2. $\dfrac{x^2 + x - 6}{x + 3}$

3. $\dfrac{x^2 - 6x + 9}{x - 3}$

4. $\dfrac{x^2 - 25}{x + 5}$

5. $\dfrac{x^2 + 2x - 9}{x - 2}$

6. $\dfrac{x^2 + 5x - 9}{x - 2}$

The Pythagorean Theorem

The Pythagorean theorem states that for any right triangle, if a and b are the lengths of the legs and c is the length of the hypotenuse, then $a^2 + b^2 = c^2$.

■ *You will need:*

■ *ruler, pencil, scissors, and graph paper*

Another way to view the theorem is to say that the sum of the areas of two squares with sides a and b is equal to the area of a square with side c. You can use this to demonstrate the theorem.

1. Draw a right triangle. Then draw three squares, one on each side of the right triangle.

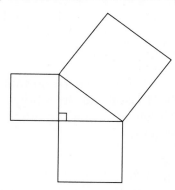

2. Mark the center of the larger of the two smaller squares. Through this point, draw one line parallel to the hypotenuse and another line perpendicular to the hypotenuse.

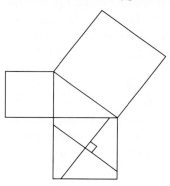

3. Cut out the two smaller squares. Cut the one you have marked into pieces outlined by the mark. Take all and fit them together on the square with the hypotenuse as its side. In this way you have demonstrated that

$$a^2 + b^2 = c^2$$

Use the method described above to prove that $a^2 + b^2 = c^2$ for each of the following triangles. Make the triangles any size that you choose. Show the constructions on a separate sheet of paper.

1. right triangle ABC where $a = b$

2. right triangle ABC where $a > b$

Penny Functions

Conduct this experiment. Place a ruler on the edge of a desk or table with the end marked zero extending over the edge. Place one penny at the last mark on the other end of the ruler. Use the point of a pencil to push the ruler toward the edge until it starts to tip over. Repeat the experiment with from 2 to 10 pennies.

■ *You will need:*

■ *centimeter ruler, pencil, and 10 pennies*

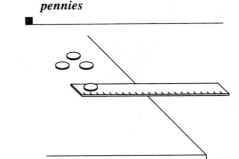

1. Record the data from the experiment in the table below.

   Let x = the number of pennies on the edge of the ruler.
   Let $f(x)$ = the distance the ruler extends over the edge rounded to the nearest tenth of a centimeter.

x	1	2	3	4	5	6	7	8	9	10
$f(x)$										

2. Make a graph showing the relationship between x and $f(x)$ in your table. Connect the points.

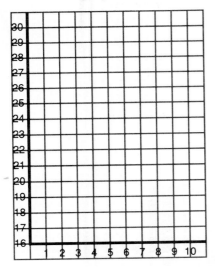

3. Is $f(x)$ increasing or decreasing with x?

4. Is the change in $f(x)$ increasing or decreasing with x?

5. Does $f(x)$ vary directly with x?

6. Does $f(x)$ vary inversely with x?

7. Is the function linear or nonlinear (curved)?

Completing the Square

You can make and use algebra tiles like those shown below to model completing the square.

■ *You will need:*

■ *algebra tiles or cardboard, ruler, and scissors*

x^2 $-x^2$ x $-x$ 1 -1

This is the procedure:

1. Model the expression with tiles.

2. Use the tiles to form two sides of a square.

3. Complete the square.

Cut the tiles into halves or fourths if necessary.

EXAMPLE 1: $x^2 + 8x$

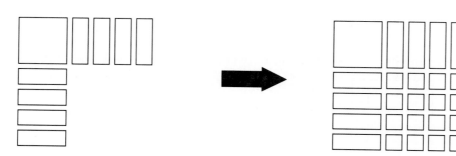

$x^2 + 8x + 16 = (x + 4)^2$

EXAMPLE 2: $x^2 - 5x$

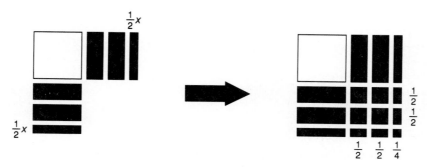

$$x^2 - 5x + 6\frac{1}{4} = \left(x - 2\frac{1}{2}\right)^2$$

Use tiles to complete the squares. Show each construction and record the trinomial as a product of squares.

1. $x^2 + 10x$ **2.** $x^2 - 8x$ **3.** $x^2 - 18x$ **4.** $x^2 + 7x$

Use tiles to complete the squares. Find all middle terms.

5. $x^2 +$ _____ $+ 36$ **6.** $4x^2 +$ _____ $+ 16$ **7.** $x^2 +$ _____ $+ 9$

MANIPULATIVE ACTIVITY 14
For use with Lesson 14-2

NAME _____

DATE _____

A Special Spiral

Make a spiral with 16 right triangles similar to
the one pictured below. Starting in the center
of a sheet of paper, draw a right triangle with
each leg 1 in. long. Then use the hypotenuse
of this triangle as a leg and draw another right
triangle with the other leg 1 in. long. Continue
in this manner to draw right triangles until
they overlap.

■ *You will need:*

■ *inch ruler, pencil, protractor,
calculator, and table of sine and
cosine functions*

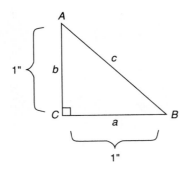

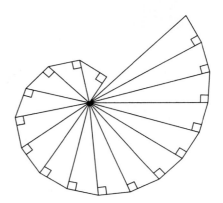

Complete the chart below for the first four triangles. Use a table of sine and cosine functions to
find the values of ∠A and ∠B. Look for a pattern as you work. Then, on another sheet of paper,
continue the chart and use the pattern to show the result for 16 triangles.

Hints: In right triangle *ABC* where *c* is the hypotenuse,

$$a^2 + b^2 = c^2 \qquad \sin A = \frac{a}{c} \qquad \cos B = \frac{a}{c}$$

	a	b	c	$\sin A$	$\angle A$	$\cos B$	$\angle B$
1	1	1	$\sqrt{2}$	$\frac{\sqrt{2}}{2}$	45°	$\frac{\sqrt{2}}{2}$	45°
2	1	$\sqrt{2}$	$\sqrt{3}$	$\frac{\sqrt{3}}{3}$	35°		
3	1						
4	1						

Hits and Misses

■ *You will need:*
■ $\frac{3}{4}''$ *inch graph paper or a grid of lines 3 units apart on $\frac{1}{4}''$ graph paper, a penny*

Imagine tossing a penny onto $\frac{3''}{4}$ graph paper like that shown below in Figure 1. If the penny covers a point of intersection, then the outcome is a "hit." Otherwise, it is a "miss."

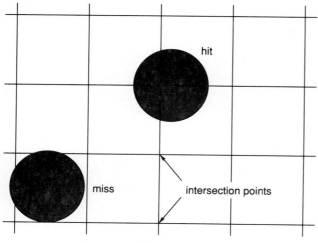

Figure 1

Figure 2

Look at Figure 2. If the center of the coin falls inside a white circle, then the coin will cover an intersection. If the center of the coin falls in a shaded area, then the coin will not cover an intersection.

1. What formula would you use to find the area of each circle in which the center of the coin must fall in order to produce a hit?

2. What is the area of each square in terms of *r*, the radius of each white circle?

3. Write the probability of a hit as a ratio of the area of a white circle to the area of a square. Simplify, if possible.

4. Using 3.14 as an approximation for π, write a decimal for the probability of a hit.

Now conduct an experiment. Toss a penny on the graph 100 times. Keep a running tally of the hits and misses.

Hits ---
_____

Misses -

5. What is the ratio of hits to tosses?

6. Does the data match the expected results?

Perform the experiment again. Combine the results with the results of your first experiment.

7. What is the ratio of hits to tosses?

8. Does the data come closer to matching the expected results?

Looking for Errors

The following 15 blackline masters contain exercises designed to develop error analysis skills in your students. The activities are appropriate for all levels of students.

On these worksheets, students check over already worked-out exercises and search for errors in the work. They identify the step containing the error and then give the correct answer. The errors, for the most part, are conceptual rather than computational.

You may want your students to give a name for each type of algebraic error that they find, for example, "dingy distribution," "combining unlike terms," "plus-minus syndrome," "fickle factoring," etc. We have included a description of each error along with the correct solution in the answers found at the end of this supplement.

The question lines and exercises are modeled after those found in the Examples, Try This, and A-level exercises in the text. The number of the lesson to which the exercises correspond is shown at the left of each direction line.

These sheets may be assigned independently as part of a chapter review. They also work well in small-group situations. Either way, they will add a new dimension to your students' understanding of algebraic concepts and enrich their critical thinking skills.

LOOKING FOR ERRORS 1

For use after Lesson 1-5

NAME _____

DATE _____

Using the Commutative, Identity, Associative, and Distributive Properties

Find the error, if any, in each exercise. Identify the step(s) in which the error(s) occur. If the exercise is correct, write, "No errors."

__1-2__ Use a commutative property to write an equivalent expression.

1. $x + 3$

$\boxed{1}\ = 3 \cdot x$

2. $xy + 7$

$\boxed{1}\ = 7y + x$

3. $4 + ab$

$\boxed{1}\ = b + a + 4$

Write an equivalent expression. Use the indicated name for 1.

4. $\frac{5}{2}$ Use $\frac{2}{2}$ for 1.

$\boxed{1}\ \frac{5}{2} = \frac{5}{2} + \frac{2}{2}$

$\boxed{2}\ = \frac{7}{2}$

5. $\frac{6}{9}$ Use $\frac{4}{4}$ for 1.

$\boxed{1}\ \frac{6}{9} = \frac{6 + 4}{9 + 4}$

$\boxed{2}\ = \frac{10}{13}$

6. $\frac{2}{3}$ Use $\frac{3}{3}$ for 1.

$\boxed{1}\ \frac{2}{3} = \frac{2}{3} \cdot \frac{3}{3}$

$\boxed{2}\ = \frac{6}{9}$

__1-4__ Use an associative property to write an equivalent expression.

7. $(a + b) + c$

$\boxed{1}\ = a + (bc)$

8. $(6 \cdot x) \cdot y$

$\boxed{1}\ = 6 + (x \cdot y)$

9. $4 \cdot (x \cdot y)$

$\boxed{1}\ = (4 \cdot x) \cdot (4 \cdot y)$

__1-5__ Use the distributive property to write an equivalent expression.

10. $2(x + 3)$

$\boxed{1}\ = 2 \cdot x + 3$

$\boxed{2}\ = 2x + 3$

11. $(x + y) \cdot 3$

$\boxed{1}\ = x + 3 \cdot y$

$\boxed{2}\ = x + 3y$

12. $9 \cdot (a + b)$

$\boxed{1}\ = 9 + a \cdot 9 + b$

$\boxed{2}\ = 9 + 9a + b$

Factor.

13. $7x + 14y$

$\boxed{1}\ = 7 \cdot (x + 7 \cdot y)$

$\boxed{2}\ = 7(x + 7y)$

14. $ax + bx$

$\boxed{1}\ = a + (b \cdot x)$

$\boxed{2}\ = a + bx$

15. $2x + 2y$

$\boxed{1}\ = 2 \cdot x + 2 \cdot y$

$\boxed{2}\ = (2 \cdot 2)(x + y)$

$\boxed{3}\ = 4(x + y)$

Collect like terms.

16. $6x + 4x^2 + 2x + 7$

$\boxed{1}\ = 4x^2 + 6x + 2x + 7$

$\boxed{2}\ = 4x^2 + (6 + 2)x^2 + 7$

$\boxed{3}\ = (4 + 8)x^2 + 7$

$\boxed{4}\ = 12x^2 + 7$

17. $2x + y + 3x + y$

$\boxed{1}\ = 2x + 3x + y + y$

$\boxed{2}\ = (2 + 3)(x \cdot x) + y + y$

$\boxed{3}\ = 5x^2 + 2y$

18. $a + b + 2a + b$

$\boxed{1}\ = ab + 2ab$

$\boxed{2}\ = (1 + 2)ab$

$\boxed{3}\ = 3ab$

50 *Algebra Enrichment*

Multiplicative Operations on Rational Numbers

Find the error, if any, in each exercise. Identify the step(s) in which the error(s) occur. If the exercise is correct, write, "No errors."

2-5   Multiply.

1. $-4(13)(-9)$

  $\boxed{1} = -4(-117)$

  $\boxed{2} = -468$

2. $7(-3)(11)$

  $\boxed{1} = 21(11)$

  $\boxed{2} = 231$

3. $-5(-2)(-12)$

  $\boxed{1} = -10(-12)$

  $\boxed{2} = 120$

4. $\dfrac{4}{5}\left(-\dfrac{2}{3}\right)\left(-\dfrac{1}{2}\right)$

  $\boxed{1} = \dfrac{4}{5}\left(-\dfrac{1}{3}\right)$

  $\boxed{2} = -\dfrac{4}{15}$

5. $\dfrac{3}{4}\left(-\dfrac{1}{4}\right)\left(\dfrac{1}{2}\right)$

  $\boxed{1} = \dfrac{3}{4}\left(\dfrac{1}{8}\right)$

  $\boxed{2} = \dfrac{3}{32}$

6. $\dfrac{1}{7}(-3)(-6)$

  $\boxed{1} = \dfrac{1}{7}(-18)$

  $\boxed{2} = -\dfrac{18}{7}$

2-6   Divide.

7. $\dfrac{1}{8} \div \dfrac{1}{7}$

  $\boxed{1} = \dfrac{8}{1} \cdot \dfrac{1}{7}$

  $\boxed{2} = \dfrac{8}{7}$

8. $\dfrac{2}{3} \div \dfrac{3}{4}$

  $\boxed{1} = \dfrac{2}{3} - \dfrac{4}{3}$

  $\boxed{2} = -\dfrac{2}{3}$

9. $\dfrac{6}{7} \div \dfrac{1}{3}$

  $\boxed{1} = \dfrac{6}{7} \div \dfrac{3}{1}$

  $\boxed{2} = \dfrac{2}{7}$

10. $\dfrac{1}{9} \div \dfrac{1}{4}$

  $\boxed{1} = \dfrac{1}{9}\left(\dfrac{1}{4}\right)$

  $\boxed{2} = \dfrac{1}{36}$

11. $\dfrac{1}{3} \div \dfrac{2}{3}$

  $\boxed{1} = \dfrac{2}{3} \cdot \dfrac{1}{3}$

  $\boxed{2} = \dfrac{2}{9}$

12. $\dfrac{2}{5} \div \dfrac{1}{4}$

  $\boxed{1} = \dfrac{5}{2} \cdot \dfrac{1}{4}$

  $\boxed{2} = \dfrac{5}{8}$

2-7   Multiply.

13. $-5(3x - 3y + 7)$

  $\boxed{1}$ $(-5)(3x) - 3y + 7$

  $\boxed{2}$ $-15x - 3y + 7$

14. $4(-3 + x - 2y)$

  $\boxed{1}$ $4(-3) + 4(x) + 4(-2y)$

  $\boxed{2}$ $-12 + 4x - 8y$

Factor.

15. $-\dfrac{1}{3}a + \dfrac{2}{3}b - 1$

  $\boxed{1}$ $-\dfrac{1}{3}(a) + \dfrac{1}{3}(2b) - \dfrac{1}{3}(3)$

  $\boxed{2}$ $-\dfrac{1}{3}(a + 2b - 3)$

16. $xy + xz - 7x$

  $\boxed{1}$ $x(y) + x(z) - 7(x)$

  $\boxed{2}$ $x(y + z) - 7x$

LOOKING FOR ERRORS 3
For use after Lesson 3-7

NAME _____

DATE _____

Solving Equations

Find the error, if any, in each exercise. Identify the step(s) in which the error(s) occur. If the exercise is correct, write, "No errors."

3-3   Solve.

1. $3x = 12$

- ⬜1 $3x - 3 = 12 - 3$
- ⬜2 $x = 9$

2. $a + 12 = 24$

- ⬜1 $(a + 12)\left(\frac{1}{12}\right) = (24)\left(\frac{1}{12}\right)$
- ⬜2 $a = 2$

3. $\frac{1}{4}z = 28$

- ⬜1 $\frac{1}{4}z \cdot \frac{1}{4} = 28 \cdot \frac{1}{4}$
- ⬜2 $z = 7$

4. $3x + 39 = 69$

- ⬜1 $3x + 39 - 39 = 69 + 39$
- ⬜2 $3x = 108$
- ⬜3 $\frac{1}{3} \cdot 3x = \frac{1}{3} \cdot 108$
- ⬜4 $x = 36$

5. $-7t + 36 = 71$

- ⬜1 $-7t + 36 - 36 = 71 - 36$
- ⬜2 $-7t = 35$
- ⬜3 $-\frac{1}{7}(-7t) = \frac{1}{7} \cdot 35$
- ⬜4 $t = 5$

6. $2x + 10x = 120$

- ⬜1 $(2 \cdot 10)x = 120$
- ⬜2 $20x = 120$
- ⬜3 $\frac{1}{20} \cdot 20x = \frac{1}{20} \cdot 120$
- ⬜4 $x = 6$

7. $6y - y = 80$

- ⬜1 $(6 - 1)y = 80$
- ⬜2 $5y = 80$
- ⬜3 $\frac{1}{5} \cdot 5y = \frac{1}{5} \cdot 80$
- ⬜4 $y = 16$

8. $4 + \frac{1}{2}m = 20$

- ⬜1 $4 + \frac{1}{2}m \cdot 2 = 20 \cdot 2$
- ⬜2 $4 + m = 40$
- ⬜3 $4 + m - 4 = 40 - 4$
- ⬜4 $m = 36$

9. $-5 + 2x = 17$

- ⬜1 $-5 + 2x - 5 = 17 - 5$
- ⬜2 $2x = 12$
- ⬜3 $\frac{1}{2} \cdot 2x = \frac{1}{2} \cdot 12$
- ⬜4 $x = 6$

3-5   Solve.

10. $2t + 2 = 3t - 61$

- ⬜1 $2t - 2t + 2 =$ $3t - 2t - 61$
- ⬜2 $2 = t - 61$
- ⬜3 $2 + 61 = t - 61 + 61$
- ⬜4 $63 = t$

11. $6y - 5 + 5y + 35 = y$

- ⬜1 $(6 + 5)y - (5 + 35) = y$
- ⬜2 $11y - 40 = y$
- ⬜3 $11y - y - 40 = y - y$
- ⬜4 $10y - 40 = 0$
- ⬜5 $10y = 40$
- ⬜6 $y = 4$

12. $5x = 10x + 50$

- ⬜1 $5x \cdot \frac{1}{5} = 10x + 50 \cdot \frac{1}{5}$
- ⬜2 $x = 10x + 10$
- ⬜3 $x - 10x =$ $10x + 10 - 10x$
- ⬜4 $-9x = 10$
- ⬜5 $x = -\frac{10}{9}$

3-7   Solve for the given variable.

13. $V = \frac{1}{3}wlh$ for h

- ⬜1 $\frac{1}{3wl} \cdot V = \frac{1}{3wl} \cdot \frac{1}{3}wlh$
- ⬜2 $\frac{V}{3wl} = h$

14. $F = \frac{mv^2}{r}$ for r

- ⬜1 $F - mv^2 = \frac{mv^2}{r} - mv^2$
- ⬜2 $F - mv^2 = \frac{1}{r}$
- ⬜3 $r = \frac{1}{F - mv^2}$

52   *Algebra Enrichment*

Working with Inequalities

Find the error, if any, in each exercise. Identify the step(s) in which the error(s) occur. If the exercise is correct, write, "No errors."

4-2 Solve and graph the solution.

1. $x + 13 < 2$

    ☐1 $x + 13 - 13 < 2 - 13$

    ☐2 $x < -11$

    ☐3

    -15 -14 -13 -12 -11 -10 -9 -8 -7 -6

2. $x - 7 \geq 16$

    ☐1 $x - 7 + 7 \geq 16 + 7$

    ☐2 $x \geq 23$

    ☐3

    18 19 20 21 22 23 24 25 26 27

3. $2y + 4 - y > 6$

    ☐1 $y + 4 > 6$

    ☐2 $y + 4 - 4 > 6 + 4$

    ☐3 $y > 10$

    ☐4

    6 7 8 9 10 11 12 13 14 15

4. $2 + 6 \leq 5n + 8 - 4n$

    ☐1 $8 \leq n + 8$

    ☐2 $8 - 8 \leq n + 8 - 8$

    ☐3 $0 \leq n$

    ☐4 $0 \leq n$

    ☐5

    -4 -3 -2 -1 0 1 2 3 4 5

4-3 Solve.

5. $-5y \leq 25$

    ☐1 $\left(-\frac{1}{5}\right)(-5y) \leq \left(-\frac{1}{5}\right)(25)$

    ☐2 $y \leq -5$

7. $-55 \geq -11x$

    ☐1 $\left(-\frac{1}{11}\right)(-55) \leq \left(-\frac{1}{11}\right)(-11x)$

    ☐2 $-5 \leq x$

6. $16x > -64$

    ☐1 $\left(\frac{1}{16}\right)16x > \left(\frac{1}{16}\right)(-64)$

    ☐2 $x < -4$

8. $6m < -54$

    ☐1 $\frac{1}{6}(6m) < \frac{1}{6}(-54)$

    ☐2 $m < -9$

4-5 Translate to an inequality.

9. Twice a number is at most 40.

    ☐1 $2x < 40$

11. Seven times a number is under 30.

    ☐1 $30 > 7y$

13. Three times a number is less than 9.

    ☐1 $3 < 9y$

10. Thirty times a number is less than 30.

    ☐1 $30n > 30$

12. A number is at most 14.

    ☐1 $x \leq 14$

14. Sixteen is less than twice a number.

    ☐1 $2x > 16$

Working With Exponents and Polynomials

Find the error, if any, in each exercise. Identify the step(s) in which the error(s) occur. If the exercise is correct, write, "No errors."

<u>5-2</u>   Simplify.

1. $(x^5)^2$

    $\boxed{1}\ = x^5 \cdot x^5$

    $\boxed{2}\ = x^{5\cdot5}$

    $\boxed{3}\ = x^{25}$

2. $(3y^2)^3$

    $\boxed{1}\ = (3y^2)(3y^2)(3y^2)$

    $\boxed{2}\ = 3 \cdot 3 \cdot 3 \cdot y^2 \cdot y^2 \cdot y^2$

    $\boxed{3}\ = 27y^6$

<u>5-8</u>   Subtract.

3. $(x^3 + 6x^2 + x) - (x^3 - 2x^2)$

    $\boxed{1}\ = (x^3 + 6x^2 + x) + (-x^3 + 2x^2)$

    $\boxed{2}\qquad x^3 + 6x^2 + x$

    $\boxed{3}\ \underline{+ (-x^3 + 2x^2 + 0)}$

    $\boxed{4}\qquad\qquad\qquad 8x^4 + x$

4. $(5x^2 + 7x + 2) - (x^2 - 3)$

    $\boxed{1}\ = (5x^2 + 7x + 2) + (x^2 + 3)$

    $\boxed{2}\qquad 5x^2 + 7x + 2$

    $\boxed{3}\ \underline{+ (\ x^2\qquad\ + 3)}$

    $\boxed{4}\qquad 6x^2 + 7x + 5$

<u>5-10</u>   Multiply.

5. $(x + 2)(x - 2)$

    $\boxed{1}\ = x(x - 2) + 2(x + 2)$

    $\boxed{2}\ = x^2 - 2x + 2x + 4$

    $\boxed{3}\ = x^2 + 4$

6. $(x + 7)^2$

    $\boxed{1}\ = (x + 7)(x + 7)$

    $\boxed{2}\ = x(x + 7) + 7(x + 7)$

    $\boxed{3}\ = x^2 + 7x + 7x + 49$

    $\boxed{4}\ = x^2 + 14x^2 + 49$

    $\boxed{5}\ = 15x^2 + 49$

7. $(2x - 3)^2$

    $\boxed{1}\ = (2x - 3)(2x - 3)$

    $\boxed{2}\ = 2x(2x - 3) - 3$

    $\boxed{3}\ = 4x^2 - 6x - 3$

<u>5-11</u>   Multiply.

8. $(x^3 + 2x^2 - 4)(x^2 + 2)$

    $\boxed{1}\ = (x^3 + 2x^2 - 4)x^2 + (x^3 + 2x^2 - 4)2$

    $\boxed{2}\ = x^5 + 2x^4 - 4x^2 + 2x^3 + 4x^2 - 8$

    $\boxed{3}\ = x^5 + 2x^4 + 2x^3 - 8$

9. $(x - 2)(x^3 + 7x + 2)$

    $\boxed{1}\ = x(x^3 + 7x + 2) - 2$

    $\boxed{2}\ = x^4 + 7x^2 + 2x - 2$

10. $(x^2 + 4)(2x - 3)$

    $\boxed{1}\ = x^2(2x - 3) + 4(2x - 3)$

    $\boxed{2}\ = 2x^3 - 3x^2 + 8x - 12$

11. $(x - 3)(x^4 + 3x - 7)$

    $\boxed{1}\ = x(x^4 + 3x - 7) - 3(x^4 + 3x - 7)$

    $\boxed{2}\ = x^5 + 3x^2 + 7x - 3x^4 + 9x - 21$

    $\boxed{3}\ = x^5 - 3x^4 + 3x^2 + 16x - 21$

LOOKING FOR ERRORS 6

For use after Lesson 6-7

NAME _____

DATE _____

Factoring Polynomial Expressions

Find the error, if any, in each exercise. Identify the step(s) in which the error(s) occur. If the exercise is correct, write, "No errors."

__6-1__   Factor.

1. $9x^2 + 9$
$\boxed{1} = 9(x^2) + 9$
$\boxed{2} = 9(x^2 + 0)$

2. $7x^2 - 21x$
$\boxed{1} = 7(x^2) - 7(3x)$
$\boxed{2} = 7(x^2 - 3x)$

3. $60a^2b - 40a^2$
$\boxed{1} = 10a^2(6b) - 10a^2(4)$
$\boxed{2} = 10a^2(6b - 4)$

__6-5__   Factor.

4. $2x^2 + 10x + 12$
$\boxed{1} = (2x + 4)(x + 3)$

5. $4x^2 - 4x - 48$
$\boxed{1} = 2(2x^2 - 2x - 24)$
$\boxed{2} = 2(2x + 6)(x - 4)$

6. $10x^2 - 10x - 20$
$\boxed{1} = 10(x^2 - x - 2)$
$\boxed{2} = 10(x - 2)(x + 1)$

7. $2x^2 + 4x - 48$
$\boxed{1} = (2x + 12)(x - 4)$

8. $7x^2 - 14x - 21$
$\boxed{1} = (x - 3)(7x + 7)$

9. $6x^2 + 30x + 36$
$\boxed{1} = 3(2x + 4)(x + 3)$

__6-6__   Factor.

10. $2x^3 - 2x^2 + 6x - 6$
$\boxed{1} = x^2(2x - 2) + 3(2x - 2)$
$\boxed{2} = (x^2 + 3)(2x - 2)$

11. $3x^3 + 3x^2 + 9x + 9$
$\boxed{1} = x^2(3x + 3) + 3(3x + 3)$
$\boxed{2} = (x^2 + 3)(3x + 3)$

12. $x^3 + 4x^2 - x - 4$
$\boxed{1} = x^2(x + 4) - 1(x + 4)$
$\boxed{2} = (x^2 - 1)(x + 4)$

__6-7__   Factor.

13. $2x^3 + 6x^2 + 4x$
$\boxed{1} = x(2x^2 + 6x + 4)$
$\boxed{2} = x(x + 2)(2x + 2)$

14. $3x^2 + 3x - 6$
$\boxed{1} = (x + 2)(3x - 3)$

15. $4x^2 - 20x + 24$
$\boxed{1} = 2(2x^2 - 10x + 12)$
$\boxed{2} = 2(2x - 4)(x - 3)$

16. $-3x^2 + 12y^2$
$\boxed{1} = 3(x^2 - 4y^2)$
$\boxed{2} = 3(x - 2y)(x + 2y)$

17. $a^2 + b^2$
$\boxed{1} = a^2 - (-b^2)$
$\boxed{2} = (a + (-b))(a - (-b))$
$\boxed{3} = (a - b)(a + b)$

18. $4p^2 - 9q^2$
$\boxed{1} = (4p + 9q)(4p - 9q)$

© Addison-Wesley Publishing Company. All rights reserved.

Algebra Enrichment   55

Finding the Slope of Graphs and Linear Equations

Find the error, if any, in each exercise. Identify the step(s) in which the error(s) occur. If the exercise is correct, write, "No errors."

7-4   Find the slopes of the lines containing these points.

1. $(3, 5), (2, -2)$

[1] $\dfrac{2 - (-2)}{3 - 5}$

[2] $= -\dfrac{4}{2}$

[3] $= -2$

[4] The slope is -2.

2. $(3, 3), (-3, -3)$

[1] $\dfrac{3 - 3}{3 - 3}$

[2] $= \dfrac{0}{0}$

[3] Since division by 0 is not defined, the line has no slope.

3. $(2, 4), (4, 2)$

[1] $\dfrac{4 - 2}{2 - 4}$

[2] $= -\dfrac{2}{2}$

[3] $= -1$

[4] The slope is -1.

7-5   Find the slope of each line by solving for y.

4. $2x - y = 4$

[1] $2x = y + 4$

[2] $x = \dfrac{1}{2}y + 2$

[3] The slope is $\dfrac{1}{2}$.

5. $4y = 3x$

[1] $y = 3x - 4$

[2] The slope is -4.

6. $2x - 6y = 37$

[1] $2x = 6y + 37$

[2] $x = 3y + \dfrac{37}{2}$

[3] The slope is 3.

7. $4y + x = 9$

[1] $4y = x + 9$

[2] $y = \dfrac{1}{4}x + \dfrac{9}{4}$

[3] The slope is $\dfrac{1}{4}$.

8. $y - x = 13$

[1] $y = x + 13$

[2] The slope is 0.

9. $6x + 2y = 10$

[1] $2y = 10 - 6x$

[2] $y = 5 - 3x$

[3] The slope is 5.

7-6   Write an equation for each line with the given slope and y-intercept.

10. $m = 3$, y-intercept of 2

[1] $y = 2x + 3$

11. $m = \dfrac{1}{3}$, y-intercept of 1

[1] $x = \dfrac{1}{3}y + 1$

12. $m = 0$, y-intercept of 0

[1] $y = 1$

Solving Simultaneous Equations

Find the error, if any, in each exercise. Identify the step(s) in which the error(s) occur. If the exercise is correct, write, "No errors."

8-2   Solve using the substitution method.

1. $x + y = 6$

$x = 4 + y$

  1. Substitute 4 for x in the first equation.
  2. $4 + y = 6$
  3. $y = 2$
  4. Substitute 2 for y in the second equation.
  5. $x = 4 + 2$
  6. $x = 6$
  7. The answer is (2, 6).

2. $2y - x = 3$

$x = y + 7$

  1. Substitute $y + 7$ for x in the first equation.
  2. $2y - y + 7 = 3$
  3. $y + 7 = 3$
  4. $y = -4$
  5. Substitute -4 for y in the second equation.
  6. $x = -4 + 7$
  7. $x = 3$
  8. The answer is (3, -4).

3. $y + 2x = 9$

$x = y - 3$

  1. Substitute $y - 3$ for x in the first equation.
  2. $y + 2y - 3 = 9$
  3. $3y - 3 = 9$
  4. $3y = 12$
  5. $y = 4$
  6. Substitute 4 for y in the second equation.
  7. $x = 4 - 3$
  8. $x = 1$
  9. The answer is (1, 4).

8-3   Solve using the addition method.

4. $x + y = 12$

$\underline{x - y = 4}$

  1. $x = 16$
  2. The answer is (16, -4).

5. $-x + y = 6$

$\underline{x + y = 2}$

  1. $y = 8$
  2. The answer is (2, 8).

6. $-x + y = 12$

$\underline{2x - y = 4}$

  1. $x = 16$
  2. The answer is (16, 28).

7. $y - x = 10$

$\underline{-y - x = 2}$

  1. $2x = 12$
  2. The answer is (6, 16).

8. $3y + x = 5$

$\underline{-2y - x = 0}$

  1. $y = 5$
  2. The answer is (-10, 5).

9. $x + y = 16$

$\underline{x - y = 2}$

  1. $x = 18$
  2. The answer is (18, -2).

Solving and Graphing Inequalities; Solving Equations with Absolute Value

Find the error, if any, in each exercise. Identify the step(s) in which the error(s) occur. If the exercise is correct, write, "No errors."

9-2   Solve and graph.

1. $2 < x + 3 \leq 3$

    ⬜1 $2 < x + 3$ and $x + 3 \leq 3$

    ⬜2 $-1 < x$ and $x \leq 0$

    ⬜3

2. $1 < x + 7 \leq 6$

    ⬜1 $1 < x + 7$ and $x + 7 \leq 6$

    ⬜2 $-6 < x$ and $x \leq -1$

    ⬜3

3. $2x < 4$ or $x + 3 < 7$

    ⬜1 $x < 2$ or $x < 4$

    ⬜2

4. $2x + 6 < 0$ or $x \geq 0$

    ⬜1 $2x < -6$ or $x \geq 0$

    ⬜2 $x < -3$ or $x \geq 0$

    ⬜3

9-3   Solve.

5. $|4x + 8| = 32$

    ⬜1 $4x + 8 = 32$ or $-4x - 8 = 32$

    ⬜2 $4x = 24$ or $-4x = 40$

    ⬜3 $x = 6$ or $x = -10$

6. $\left|\dfrac{1}{3}x - 2\right| = 6$

    ⬜1 $\dfrac{1}{3}x - 2 = 6$ or $\dfrac{1}{3}x + 2 = 6$

    ⬜2 $\dfrac{1}{3}x = 8$ or $\dfrac{1}{3}x = 4$

    ⬜3 $x = 24$ or $x = 12$

7. $|3x + 2| = 14$

    ⬜1 $3x + 2 = 14$ or $3x + 2 = -14$

    ⬜2 $3x = 12$ or $3x = -16$

    ⬜3 $x = 4$ or $x = -\dfrac{16}{3}$

8. $|9x - 4| = 14$

    ⬜1 $9x - 4 = 14$

    ⬜2 $9x = 18$

    ⬜3 $x = 2$

9-5   **9.** Determine whether $(0, 0)$ is a solution of $x - y < 0$.

    ⬜1 Test the point $(0, 0)$.

    ⬜2 $0 - 0 = 0$

    ⬜3 Yes

10. Determine whether $\left(\dfrac{1}{2}, -\dfrac{1}{4}\right)$ is a solution of $7y + 9x > -3$.

    ⬜1 $7\left(\dfrac{1}{2}\right) + 9\left(-\dfrac{1}{4}\right) = \dfrac{5}{4}$

    ⬜2 $\dfrac{5}{4} > -3$

    ⬜3 Yes

Working with Rational Expressions; Dividing Polynomials

Find the error, if any, in each exercise. Identify the step(s) in which the error(s) occur. If the exercise is correct, write, "No errors."

10-1   Simplify.

1. $\dfrac{x^2 + 2x + 1}{x^2 - 1}$

$\boxed{1} = \dfrac{x^2 + 2x + 1}{x^2 - 1}$

$\boxed{2} = \dfrac{2x + 1}{-1}$

$\boxed{3} = -2x - 1$

2. $\dfrac{x^2 + 7x + 12}{x + 3}$

$\boxed{1} = \dfrac{x(x + 7) + 12}{x + 3}$

$\boxed{2} = \dfrac{(x + 7) + 12}{+3}$

$\boxed{3} = \dfrac{x + 19}{3}$

3. $\dfrac{x^2 - 2x + 374}{x^2 - 2x + 374}$

$\boxed{1} = \dfrac{1}{1}$

$\boxed{2} = 1$

10-4   Add and simplify.

4. $\dfrac{7a}{b} + \dfrac{4a}{b}$

$\boxed{1} = \dfrac{7a + 4a}{b + b}$

$\boxed{2} = \dfrac{11a}{2b}$

5. $\dfrac{3x}{y} + \dfrac{7}{y}$

$\boxed{1} = \dfrac{3x + 7}{y}$

$\boxed{2} = \dfrac{10x}{y}$

6. $\dfrac{4x}{6} + \dfrac{3x}{6}$

$\boxed{1} = \dfrac{4x + 3x}{6}$

$\boxed{2} = \dfrac{7x^2}{6}$

10-5   Add or subtract. Simplify.

7. $\dfrac{6}{a} + \dfrac{a}{a^2}$

$\boxed{1} = \dfrac{6}{a} \cdot \dfrac{2}{2} + \dfrac{a}{a^2}$

$\boxed{2} = \dfrac{12}{a^2} + \dfrac{a}{a^2}$

$\boxed{3} = \dfrac{12 + a}{a^2}$

8. $\dfrac{3}{a} - \dfrac{7}{a^2}$

$\boxed{1} = \dfrac{3}{a} \cdot \dfrac{a}{a} - \dfrac{7}{a^2}$

$\boxed{2} = \dfrac{3a}{a^2} - \dfrac{7}{a^2}$

$\boxed{3} = \dfrac{3a - 7}{a^2}$

9. $x + \dfrac{10}{x}$

$\boxed{1} = x \cdot \dfrac{x}{x} + \dfrac{10}{x}$

$\boxed{2} = \dfrac{x^2}{x} + \dfrac{10}{x}$

$\boxed{3} = \dfrac{x^2 + 10}{x}$

10-9   Divide.

10. $(x^2 - 1) \div (x + 1)$

$\boxed{5} \quad \begin{array}{r} x - 1 \\ x + 1 \overline{)x^2 + 0x - 1} \end{array}$

$\boxed{1} \quad \underline{x^2 + x}$

$\boxed{2} \quad -x - 1$

$\boxed{3} \quad \underline{-x - 1}$

$\boxed{4} \quad 0$

11. $(x^2 + x - 6) \div (x - 2)$

$\boxed{5} \quad \begin{array}{r} x - 1 \ \text{R} -8 \\ x - 2 \overline{)x^2 + x - 6} \end{array}$

$\boxed{1} \quad \underline{x^2 - 2x}$

$\boxed{2} \quad -x - 6$

$\boxed{3} \quad \underline{-x + 2}$

$\boxed{4} \quad -8$

LOOKING FOR ERRORS 11
For use after Lesson 11-7

NAME _____

DATE _____

Radical Expressions and Applying the Pythagorean Theorem

Find the error, if any, in each exercise. Identify the step(s) in which the error(s) occur. If the exercise is correct, write, ''No errors.''

<u>11-4</u>   Multiply and simplify.

1. $\sqrt{7} \cdot \sqrt{x}$

$\boxed{1} = \sqrt{7x \cdot 7x}$

$\boxed{2} = \sqrt{49x^2}$

$\boxed{3} = 7x$

2. $\sqrt{5} \cdot \sqrt{5}$

$\boxed{1} = \sqrt{5 \cdot 5}$

$\boxed{2} = \sqrt{25}$

$\boxed{3} = 5$

3. $\sqrt{\frac{1}{2}} \cdot \sqrt{\frac{3}{2}}$

$\boxed{1} = \sqrt{\frac{1}{2} \cdot \frac{3}{2}}$

$\boxed{2} = \sqrt{\frac{4}{2}}$

$\boxed{3} = 2$

4. $\sqrt{2} \cdot \sqrt{x+1}$

$\boxed{1} = \sqrt{2 \cdot x + 1}$

$\boxed{2} = \sqrt{2x + 1}$

<u>11-5</u>   Divide and simplify.

5. $\dfrac{\sqrt{3}}{\sqrt{9}}$

$\boxed{1} = \dfrac{\sqrt{3}}{3}$

$\boxed{2} = \sqrt{\dfrac{3}{3}}$

$\boxed{3} = \sqrt{1}$

$\boxed{4} = 1$

6. $\dfrac{\sqrt{20x^2}}{\sqrt{10}}$

$\boxed{1} = \sqrt{\dfrac{20x^2}{10}}$

$\boxed{2} = \sqrt{2x^2}$

$\boxed{3} = x^2\sqrt{2}$

7. $\dfrac{\sqrt{80x}}{\sqrt{5x}}$

$\boxed{1} = \sqrt{\dfrac{80x}{5x}}$

$\boxed{2} = \sqrt{16}$

$\boxed{3} = 4$

8. $\dfrac{\sqrt{5}}{\sqrt{3}}$

$\boxed{1} = \dfrac{\sqrt{5}}{\sqrt{3}} \cdot \dfrac{\sqrt{3}}{\sqrt{3}}$

$\boxed{2} = \dfrac{\sqrt{15}}{9}$

$\boxed{3} = \dfrac{1}{9}\sqrt{15}$

<u>11-6</u>   Add or subtract.

9. $2\sqrt{3} + 5\sqrt{3}$

$\boxed{1} = 7\sqrt{3+3}$

$\boxed{2} = 7\sqrt{6}$

10. $\sqrt{5} + \sqrt{20}$

$\boxed{1} = \sqrt{5 + 20}$

$\boxed{2} = \sqrt{25}$

$\boxed{3} = 5$

11. $\sqrt{16x-16} - \sqrt{9x-9}$

$\boxed{1} = \sqrt{16x-16-9x+9}$

$\boxed{2} = \sqrt{7x - 7}$

12. $16\sqrt{y} - \sqrt{y}$

$\boxed{1} = \sqrt{y}(16 - 0)$

$\boxed{2} = \sqrt{y}(16)$

$\boxed{3} = 16\sqrt{y}$

<u>11-7</u>   Find the length of the third side of each right triangle.

13.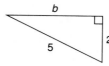

$\boxed{1}\ \ 5^2 + 2^2 = b^2$

$\boxed{2}\ \ 25 + 4 = b^2$

$\boxed{3}\ \ 29 = b^2$

$\boxed{4}\ \ b = \sqrt{29}$

14.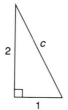

$\boxed{1}\ \ 1^2 + 2^2 = c^2$

$\boxed{2}\ \ 1 + 4 = c^2$

$\boxed{3}\ \ 5 = c^2$

$\boxed{4}\ \ c = \sqrt{5}$

15.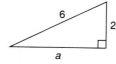

$\boxed{1}\ \ a^2 = 2^2 - 6^2$

$\boxed{2}\ \ a^2 = 4 - 36$

$\boxed{3}\ \ a^2 = -32$

$\boxed{4}\ \ a = \sqrt{-32}$

Algebra Enrichment

Relations and Functions

Find the error, if any, in each exercise. Identify the step(s) in which the error(s) occur. If the exercise is correct, write, "No errors."

12-1   Find the indicated outputs of these functions.

1. $h(x) = 7x - 12$; find $h(2)$, $h(9)$, $h(16)$, and $h(23)$.

1	$h(2) = 7x - 12$	$h(9) = 7x - 12$	$h(16) = 7x - 12$	$h(23) = 7x - 12$
2	$2 = 7x - 12$	$9 = 7x - 12$	$16 = 7x - 12$	$23 = 7x - 12$
3	$2 + 12 = 7x$	$9 + 12 = 7x$	$16 + 12 = 7x$	$23 + 12 = 7x$
4	$14 = 7x$	$21 = 7x$	$28 = 7x$	$35 = 7x$
5	$2 = x$	$3 = x$	$4 = x$	$5 = x$

12-2   **2.** Graph the function $g(x) = 2x - 3$ where the domain is the set of real numbers.

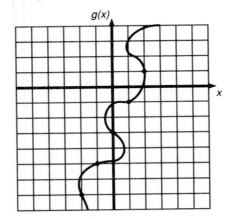

x	$g(x)$
-2	-7
-1	-5
0	-3
1	-1
2	1

12-6   Find an equation of variation.

3. The brightness of a light varies inversely with the distance from which the light is viewed. If the light has a brightness of 0.17 when seen from 1 mile, how bright would it appear from 3 miles?

1 Let B = Brightness and D = Distance.

2 Then $B = \dfrac{k}{D}$

3 $0.17 = \dfrac{k}{1}$

4 $k = 0.17$

5 The equation of variation is $B = \dfrac{0.17}{D}$

6 Substitute 4 for D and solve for B.

7 $B = \dfrac{0.17}{4}$

8 $B = 0.0425$

9 The light's brightness from 4 miles would be 0.0425.

Solving Quadratic Equations

Find the error, if any, in each exercise. Identify the step(s) in which the error(s) occur. If the exercise is correct, write, "No errors."

Solve.

13-1

1. $x^2 + x = 6$
 ☐1 $x(x + 1) = 6$
 ☐2 $x = 6$ or $x + 1 = 6$
 ☐3 $x = 6$ or 5

2. $x^2 + 20x = 0$
 ☐1 $x(x + 20) = 0$
 ☐2 $x = 0$ or $x + 20 = 0$
 ☐3 $x = 0$ or -20

3. $x^2 + 2x - 8 = 0$
 ☐1 $(x + 4)(x - 2) = 0$
 ☐2 $x = 4$ or -2

13-2

4. $(x + 6)^2 = 16$
 ☐1 $x + 6 = \sqrt{16}$
 ☐2 $x + 6 = 4$
 ☐3 $x = -2$

5. $(x + 3)^2 = 9$
 ☐1 $x + 3 = \pm\sqrt{9}$
 ☐2 $x + 3 = \pm 3$
 ☐3 $x + 3 = 3$ or -3
 ☐4 $x = 0$ or -6

6. $-5x^2 - 1 = -1$
 ☐1 $-5x^2 = -2$
 ☐2 $x^2 = \dfrac{2}{5}$
 ☐3 $x = \pm\sqrt{\dfrac{2}{5}}$
 ☐4 $x = \pm\sqrt{\dfrac{2}{5} \cdot \dfrac{5}{5}}$
 ☐5 $x = \pm\dfrac{\sqrt{10}}{5}$

13-3 Solve by completing the square.

7. $x^2 + 6x - 4 = 0$
 ☐1 $x^2 + 6x = 4$
 ☐2 $x^2 + 6x + 9 = 4 + 9$
 ☐3 $(x + 3)^2 = 13$
 ☐4 $x + 3 = \sqrt{13}$
 ☐5 $x = \sqrt{13} - 3$

8. $x^2 - 8x + 1 = 0$
 ☐1 $x^2 - 8x = -1$
 ☐2 $x^2 - 8x + 10 = -1 + 10$
 ☐3 $(x - 4)^2 = 9$
 ☐4 $x - 4 = \pm\sqrt{9}$
 ☐5 $x - 4 = 3$ or
   $x - 4 = -3$
 ☐6 $x = 7$ or 1

9. $x^2 + 2x - 1 = 0$
 ☐1 $x^2 + 2x = 1$
 ☐2 $x^2 + 2x + 1 = 1 + 1$
 ☐3 $(x + 1)^2 = 2$
 ☐4 $x + 1 = \pm\sqrt{2}$
 ☐5 $x = \pm\sqrt{2} - 1$

13-6 Solve this radical equation.

10. $\sqrt{19 - 6x} + 5 = x + 3$
 ☐1 $\sqrt{19 - 6x} = x - 2$
 ☐2 $(\sqrt{19 - 6x})^2 = (x - 2)^2$
 ☐3 $19 - 6x = x^2 - 4x + 4$
 ☐4 $0 = x^2 + 2x - 15$
 ☐5 $0 = (x + 5)(x - 3)$
 ☐6 $x + 5 = 0$ or $x - 3 = 0$
 ☐7 $x = -5$ or $x = 3$

Similar Triangles

Find the error, if any, in each exercise. Identify the step(s) in which the error(s) occur. If the exercise is correct, write, "No errors."

14-1 Find the indicated length for each pair of similar triangles.

1. $\triangle ABC \sim \triangle DGE$; find a.

$\boxed{1}$ $\dfrac{6}{12} = \dfrac{a}{3\sqrt{5}}$

$\boxed{2}$ $3\sqrt{5} \cdot \dfrac{6}{12} = \dfrac{a}{3\sqrt{5}} \cdot 3\sqrt{5}$

$\boxed{3}$ $\dfrac{6\sqrt{5}}{4} = a$

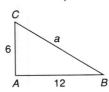

2. $\triangle ABC \sim \triangle XWZ$; find b.

$\boxed{1}$ $\dfrac{b}{4\sqrt{2}} = \dfrac{3\sqrt{2}}{8}$

$\boxed{2}$ $4\sqrt{2} \cdot \dfrac{b}{4\sqrt{2}} = \dfrac{3\sqrt{2}}{8} \cdot 4\sqrt{2}$

$\boxed{3}$ $b = \dfrac{3\sqrt{2} \cdot \sqrt{2}}{2}$

$\boxed{4}$ $b = \dfrac{3(2)}{2}$

$\boxed{5}$ $b = 3$

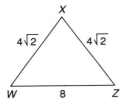

3. $\triangle ABC \sim \triangle HYG$; find h.

$\boxed{1}$ $\dfrac{6}{4} = \dfrac{h}{2\sqrt{5}}$

$\boxed{2}$ $2\sqrt{5} \cdot \dfrac{6}{4} = \dfrac{h}{2\sqrt{5}} \cdot 2\sqrt{5}$

$\boxed{3}$ $3\sqrt{5} = h$

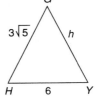

4. $\triangle ABC \sim \triangle GHI$; find a.

$\boxed{1}$ $\dfrac{5}{10} = \dfrac{a}{\sqrt{29}}$

$\boxed{2}$ $\sqrt{29} \cdot \dfrac{5}{10} = \dfrac{a}{\sqrt{29}} \cdot \sqrt{29}$

$\boxed{3}$ $\dfrac{5\sqrt{29}}{10} = a$

$\boxed{4}$ $a = \dfrac{\sqrt{29}}{2}$

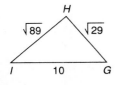

5. $\triangle ABC \sim \triangle DGE$; find b.

$\boxed{1}$ $\dfrac{10}{8} = \dfrac{b}{5\sqrt{2}}$

$\boxed{2}$ $5\sqrt{2} \cdot \dfrac{10}{8} = \dfrac{b}{5\sqrt{2}} \cdot 5\sqrt{2}$

$\boxed{3}$ $\dfrac{50\sqrt{2}}{8} = b$

$\boxed{4}$ $b = \dfrac{25\sqrt{2}}{4}$

6. $\triangle ABC \sim \triangle DFG$; find b.

$\boxed{1}$ $\dfrac{b}{4\sqrt{2}} = \dfrac{7}{2\sqrt{29}}$

$\boxed{2}$ $4\sqrt{2} \cdot \dfrac{b}{4\sqrt{2}} = \dfrac{7}{2\sqrt{29}} \cdot 4\sqrt{2}$

$\boxed{3}$ $b = \dfrac{28\sqrt{2}}{2\sqrt{29}}$

$\boxed{4}$ $b = \dfrac{14\sqrt{2}}{\sqrt{29}} \cdot \dfrac{\sqrt{29}}{\sqrt{29}}$

$\boxed{5}$ $b = \dfrac{14\sqrt{58}}{29}$

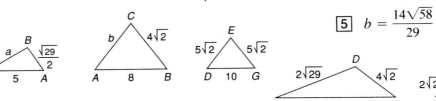

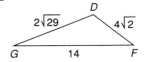

Probability and Statistics

Find the error, if any, in each exercise. Identify the step(s) in which the error(s) occur. If the exercise is correct, write, "No errors."

15-2   Find the probability.

1. One die is tossed. What is the probability that an even number will be rolled?

[1] $P(\text{even}) = P(2) + P(4) + P(6)$

[2] $= 2 + 4 + 6$

[3] $= 12$

2. What is the probability of spinning a number less than four or an odd number on a spinner showing the ten whole numbers from 1 to 10?

[1] $P(<4) + P(\text{odd}) = P(1) + P(2) + P(3) + P(1) + P(3) + P(5) + P(7) + P(9)$

[2] $= \dfrac{1}{10} + \dfrac{1}{10} + \dfrac{1}{10} + \dfrac{1}{10} + \dfrac{1}{10} + \dfrac{1}{10} + \dfrac{1}{10} + \dfrac{1}{10}$

[3] $= \dfrac{8}{10}, \text{ or } \dfrac{4}{5}$

15-4, 15-5

3. Shown below is a stem-and-leaf diagram of the low temperatures, in degrees Fahrenheit, in Dayton, Ohio, for a ten-day period. Construct a histogram.

Stem	Leaf
0	5, 7
1	2, 4, 4, 6
2	8, 8, 8
3	0

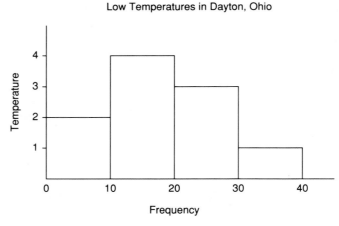

Low Temperatures in Dayton, Ohio

15-6   Find the measures of central tendency.

4. Find the mean, median, and mode for the following data.

1, 7, 6, 8, 7, 4, 2, 5, 9, 12, 3

[1] Mean: The number 7 occurs twice; it is the mean.

[2] Median: The number 4 is the middle number; it is the median.

[3] Mode: There are 11 numbers, and their sum is 64; the mode is $\dfrac{64}{11}, \text{ or } 5\dfrac{9}{11}$.

Probability/Statistics Worksheets

The following 7 blackline masters are group-activity worksheets designed to enhance student learning about probability and statistics. Some of the activities require research outside of the classroom. The compilation of the collected data occurs within the classroom.

Using each worksheet, students will learn useful probability and statistical skills that are not taught elsewhere in the textbook. The activities are designed to make math enjoyable and to develop the concept of theoretical probability through experimentation.

Each worksheet requires collecting or organizing data and analyzing and making predictions based on the results. The worksheets are self contained and first-year algebra probability skills are assumed.

Random Sample

The Fun City Magazine Company randomly places one of nine different Fun Stickers in each copy of its magazine. How many copies of the magazine do you think you would have to buy in order to obtain all nine stickers?

Kinds of Stickers

C = Cartoon sticker	N = Nature sticker	F = Friendship sticker
A = Animal sticker	O = Ocean sticker	W = Water sticker
S = Star sticker	H = School sticker	M = Mountain sticker

The table below shows the results of 10 trials. A trial ends when you have at least one of each kind of sticker. The numbers represent the numbers of copies of the magazine with each kind of sticker.

Trial	C	N	F	A	O	W	S	H	M	Total
1	1	5	7	3	2	2	4	7	8	39
2	3	2	1	2	7	3	6	6	2	32
3	1	2	3	2	3	2	7	6	7	33
4	3	2	2	3	1	3	3	4	8	29
5	3	3	8	4	3	1	1	3	2	29
6	2	2	1	3	2	2	2	1	5	20
7	1	3	3	5	1	2	3	4	7	29
8	3	2	2	4	3	1	8	6	5	34
9	2	3	5	4	4	1	3	8	5	25
10	2	3	1	3	1	3	2	6	7	28
										298

From this experiment, the number of copies of the magazine that you would expect you must buy in order to get all nine stickers is given by the following:

$$\text{expected number} = \frac{\text{total number of copies}}{\text{number of trials}}$$

$$= \frac{298}{10}$$

$$= 29.8$$

You would expect that you would have to buy about 30 copies of the magazine in order to get all nine stickers.

Conduct a similar experiment by finding and using your own sample data. Examples of experiments could include the following.

1. How many people in a crowd do you expect to have blue eyes?

2. Out of all the cars that pass a given spot during a certain period of time, how many do you expect to be red?

3. How many people in a group do you expect to tell you that green is their favorite color?

Dice Games—A Class Activity

You will need a partner for this game. Before you begin, choose which one of you will have "evens" and which one will have "odds." To play the game, you and your partner take turns rolling a pair of dice. After each roll, add the numbers on the faces of the dice. If the sum is even, then the person who has "evens" wins. If the sum is odd, then the person who has "odds" wins. Keep a tally of the wins for evens and for odds. Play the game at least twenty times.

1. Before you begin, predict who you think will have the most wins after twenty rolls of the dice.

2. Now play the game and record by tallying the wins for evens and the wins for odds in the table below.

   EVEN wins = _____

   ODD wins =

3. Was your prediction correct?

4. Did you think the same person would always win? Why or why not?

5. Combine the results of the class, and calcualte the class's experimental probability of rolling an odd sum and an even sum.

   P(odd sum) = _____   P(even sum) = _____

6. Now fill in the table below with the sums that can be rolled with two dice.

   Numbers on Die 1

	1	2	3	4	5	6
1						
2						
3						
4						
5						
6						

   Numbers on Die 2

   Use the results in the table to help find the theoretical probability of rolling an odd sum and rolling an even sum.

   P(odd sum) = _____   P(even sum) = _____

7. Does each player have an equally likely chance to win?

8. Make up another dice game. Create rules so that both players have an equally likely chance to win.

Happy Birthday—A Class Activity

What do you think the probability is that two people in your class have the same birthday?

Take a survey of your class and record the results in the table below. For example, if someone's birthday is March 4, record a 4 in the column for March.

Jan	Feb	Mar	Apr	May	Jun	Jul	Aug	Sep	Oct	Nov	Dec

Did at least two people share the same birthday?

According to the results of your survey, what is the probability that

1. someone has a birthday in January?

2. someone has a birthday before June?

3. someone has a birthday on June 24?

4. someone has a birthday on February 29?

5. someone has a birthday in a month with 30 days?

6. someone has a birthday in a month that begins with an A?

Make up a probability question of your own that can be answered by using the data in your survey.

EXTRA: Did you know that two Presidents of the United States had the same birthday? Who were they?

Did you know that three Presidents of the United States died on July 4th? Who were they?

PROBABILITY/STATISTICS 4

For use after Lesson 15-3

NAME _____

DATE _____

Sticky-Dot Dice—A Class Activity

Take one die of a pair of dice and place a
sticky dot over the face with six pips. Take
the other die and place a sticky dot over the
face with three pips. Let each sticky dot
represent the number 0.

1. Predict the sum that you think will appear
   most frequently when you roll this pair of
   dice 50 times.

2. Now test your prediction. Roll the dice 50
   times. After each roll, put a tally mark in
   the table at the right beside the sum that
   you rolled.

3. Based on the results shown in your table,
   what is the experimental probability for
   each sum?

Possible Sums	Tally
0	
1	
2	
3	
4	
5	
6	
7	
8	
9	
10	
11	

   $P(0) =$ _____ $P(6) =$ _____

   $P(1) =$ _____ $P(7) =$ _____

   $P(2) =$ _____ $P(8) =$ _____

   $P(3) =$ _____ $P(9) =$ _____

   $P(4) =$ _____ $P(10) =$ _____

   $P(5) =$ _____ $P(11) =$ _____

4. Work together in groups of four. Take each of your results from the preceding experiment and
   combine them. Record the total number of rolls for each possible sum in the table below.

Possible sums	0	1	2	3	4	5	6	7	8	9	10	11
Total rolls												

5. Using the results of your group, calculate the experimental probability for the possible sums.

   $P(0) =$ _____ $P(3) =$ _____ $P(6) =$ _____ $P(9) =$ _____

   $P(1) =$ _____ $P(4) =$ _____ $P(7) =$ _____ $P(10) =$ _____

   $P(2) =$ _____ $P(5) =$ _____ $P(8) =$ _____ $P(11) =$ _____

   Compare these experimental probabilities with those you found using the data collected on
   your own. (See Exercise 3.)

6. Make a table or draw a tree diagram to help you calculate the theoretical probability for each
   possible sum. Then compare the theoretical probabilities with the experimental probabilities
   for your group. How close are they? Do you think that combining your group's results with
   other groups will change this comparison? Explain.

Average Temperature—A Class Activity

1. The chart at the right shows daily temperatures for two days in a number of the major cities in the United States. Work together in small groups. Make a stem-and-leaf diagram for today's high temperatures.

2. Write a one-paragraph description of the information shown in the stem-and-leaf diagram. For example, tell which cities have similar temperatures, which ones have the most different temperatures, etc.

3. Determine the measures of central tendency for the set of data. Then tell which city or cities have the mean temperature, which have the median temperature, and which have the mode. In your group discuss which of these measures best reflects the average temperature for this day.

	Yesterday Hi/Lo	Today Hi/Lo		Yesterday Hi/Lo	Today Hi/Lo
Albany, NY	79/65	80/64	Juneau, AK	53/47	58/44
Albuquerque, NM	88/55	89/55	Louisville, KY	85/67	85/70
Amarillo, TX	84/59	75/55	Memphis, TN	91/74	88/74
Anchorage, AK	55/46	60/44	Miami Beach, FL	83/78	87/78
Atlanta, GA	92/71	90/71	Nashville, TN	89/69	88/69
Atlantic City, NJ	80/68	77/69	New Orleans, LA	90/72	88/71
Austin, TX	78/67	86/68	New York City, NY	78/69	76/65
Baltimore, MD	87/68	87/68	Omaha, NE	74/61	74/54
Billings, MT	63/43	75/45	Orlando, FL	95/70	91/71
Boise, ID	73/36	85/45	Philadelphia, PA	86/72	86/68
Boston, MA	64/54	63/55	Phoenix, AZ	105/78	107/77
Buffalo, NY	84/63	77/65	Pittsburgh, PA	82/75	80/66
Charleston, WV	85/62	84/67	Portland, ME	63/54	62/53
Cheyenne, WY	69/40	75/39	Portland, OR	78/45	89/50
Chicago, IL	81/66	76/62	Providence, RI	75/67	70/58
Cincinnati, OH	84/65	83/71	Raleigh, NC	91/66	89/66
Cleveland, OH	86/64	82/69	Richmond, VA	87/66	89/67
Columbus, OH	84/63	81/72	St. Louis, MO	90/66	80/68
Denver, CO	77/46	78/46	Salt Lake City, UT	73/45	80/48
Des Moines, IA	75/61	74/52	San Antonio, TX	87/66	89/67
Detroit, MI	82/64	78/66	Seattle, WA	70/48	81/50
El Paso, TX	97/59	96/61	Spokane, WA	67/36	78/42
Fairbanks, AK	66/50	63/50	Syracuse, NY	80/65	79/63
Hartford, CT	81/68	77/60	Topeka, KS	83/65	78/58
Helena, MT	62/42	74/36	Tucson, AZ	100/65	102/67
Honolulu, HI	86/66	86/68	Tulsa, OK	88/73	78/64
Houston, TX	86/73	87/72	Washington, DC	89/68	88/70
Indianapolis, IN	88/67	82/68	Wichita, KS	88/66	79/58

4. Using information from your local newspaper, radio, or television, make a record of the daily high and low temperatures in your area for one month. Also, each day during class, measure and record the temperature outside. When you have gathered the three sets of data for one month, construct three line plots. Show the data using three different colors or three different kinds of lines, such as solid, dotted, and broken lines.

5. How does the plot of the measurements taken during the class period compare with the plots for the highs and lows? Do the class measurements represent the average temperature in your area each day? Explain.

6. Find the mean, median, and mode for each set of data. Which do you think best reflects the daily average temperature? Why?

Mean, Median, and Mode—A Class Activity

Work together in small groups to find the following sets of numbers.

1. Find a set of five nonnegative integers such that their mean is 5, their median is 5, and their mode is 7.

2. Collect the solutions to Exercise 1 from all the groups in the class. Do you think that the class has found all of the possible sets of five such integers? Why do you think this?

3. How many possible sets of five nonnegative integers will satisfy the conditions given in Exercise 1? Explain how you arrived at your answer and why you think that it is correct.

4. What is the probability that the set of five integers that satisfy the conditions in Exercise 1 will contain

   a. one seven?   **b.** two sevens?   **c.** three sevens?

   d. four sevens?   **e.** five sevens?

For the following exercises, each set of numbers consists of five integers such that $0 \le N \le 20$. Find a set of numbers that satisfies the given conditions. Be sure to calculate each measure of central tendency to verify your solution. Be prepared to explain how you found the set.

5. The mean, median, and mode are equal.

6. The mean is greater than both the median and the mode.

7. The mean is less than both the median and the mode.

8. The mode is greater than the mean but is less than the median.

9. The difference between the mean and the median is greater for this set than for any other possible set.

NAME _____

DATE _____

Wink Count—A Class Activity

Work together with three or four other students to do this activity.

1. Each person will wink his or her right eye for one minute. He or she will count the winks and record the result in the following table.

Person	1	2	3	4	5
Winks					

2. Find the measures of central tendency for the data.

   Median = _____ Mean = _____ Mode = _____

3. Which person in your group is closest to having the median?

4. Suppose another person joins your group. How many times would this person have to wink in one minute to raise the mean by 10 winks?

5. Collect the results from all of the other groups in the class. Combine the results and find the measures of central tendency.

   Median = _____ Mean = _____ Mode = _____

6. Now have each person wink his or her left eye. Collect the results from all the groups in the class and find the measures of central tendency.

   Median = _____ Mean = _____ Mode = _____

   Was there any difference between the figures for the right eye and those for the left eye?

EXTRA Work with your group to solve the following problems.

7. The Dragons, a baseball team, have played 15 games so far this season, averaging 2.8 runs per game. Last season, they averaged 3.0 runs per game. They have 3 games remaining on their schedule. How many runs must they score in these games so that their average for this season will be at least as good as their average for last season? Show three different ways they might score this number of runs in 3 games. How many more ways are there, if any?

Answers

BONUS TOPIC 1
1. Yes **2.** Yes **3.** No **4.** Yes **5.** Yes **6.** 32
7. 81 **8.** $\frac{8}{125}$ **9.** $2*(3*2) = 512$, but $(2*3)*2 = 64$
10. 8 **11.** 2 **12.** No **13.** Yes **14.** No **15.** 25
16. 25 **17.** A^2

BONUS TOPIC 2
1. 1 **2.** 6 **3.** 4 **4.** 12 **5.** 8
6. 4 **7.** 10 **8.** 1 **9.** 8
10. (see right) **11.** 2 or 4
12. 1, 2, 3, or 4 **13.** 2 **14.** 7
15. 1, 3, or 5 **16.** 5
17. 10 or 20 **18.** 12, 24, 48, or 16
19. p **20.** p **21.** $p - 2$

10.

	1	2	3	4
1	1	2	3	4
2	2	4	2	4
3	3	2	1	4
4	4	4	4	4

BONUS TOPIC 3
There are 31 parakeets in the Lizard City Zoo.

BONUS TOPIC 4
1. Reflexive and transitive **2.** Symmetric **3.** Symmetric
4. Reflexive, symmetric, and transitive; an equivalence relation
5. Transitive **6.** Reflexive, symmetric, and transitive; an
equivalence relation **7.** Symmetric **8.** Reflexive and
transitive **9.** Symmetric and transitive **10.** Symmetric and
transitive **11.** Reflexive, symmetric, and transitive; an
equivalence relation **12.** Reflexive, symmetric, and transitive;
an equivalence relation.

BONUS TOPIC 5
1. $x^6 + 6x^5y + 15x^4y^2 + 20x^3y^3 + 15x^2y^4 + 6xy^5 + y^6$
2. $m^7 + 7m^6n + 21m^5n^2 + 35m^4n^3 + 35m^3n^4 + 21m^2n^5 + 7mn^6 + n^7$ **3.** $a^8 + 8a^7b + 28a^6b^2 + 56a^5b^3 + 70a^4b^4 + 56a^3b^5 + 28a^2b^6 + 8ab^7 + b^8$ **4.** $p^3 + 6p^2 + 12p + 8$
5. $c^8 + 12c^6 + 54c^4 + 108c^2 + 81$ **6.** m^{21} **7.** $55a^{30}$
8. $42p^6$

BONUS TOPIC 6
1. $19(17x + 7)$ **2.** $60(10m + 7)$ **3.** $21(13x + 3)$
4. $47(3p - 19)$ **5.** $51(21s + 17)$ **6.** $13(21w - 23)$
7. $7(169x - 70)$ **8.** $113(4a + 5)$

BONUS TOPIC 7

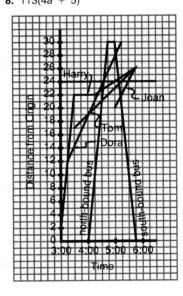

The travels of the four suspects are plotted on the graph shown
above. The only person to arrive at Mrs. Quadrant's between the
time the bus arrived in Abscissa and the time the bus arrived
back in Origin was Harry, who must have stolen the cheesecake.

BONUS TOPIC 8 (Answers will vary for 1–4.)
1. (3, 1) **2.** (6, 3) **3.** (48, 2) **4.** (13, 5)
5. one 22¢-stamp, eight 14¢-stamps

BONUS TOPIC 9
1.

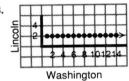

2.

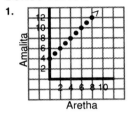

3.

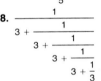

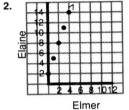

4. (3, −2), (3, −1), (3, 0),
(4, −2), (4, −1), (4, 0)
5. (−10, 8), (−9, 8),
(−8, 8), (−10, 7), (−9, 7),
(−8, 7) **6.** (−1, 2), (0, 2),
(1, 2), (−2, 1), (−1, 1),
(0, 1), (1, 1), (2, 1), (−2, 0),
(−1, 0), (0, 0), (1, 0), (2, 0),
(−2, −1), (−1, −1),
(0, −1), (1, −1), (2, −1),
(−1, −2), (0, −2), (1, −2)

BONUS TOPIC 10
1. $\frac{2}{7}$ **2.** $\frac{16}{131}$ **3.** $\frac{68}{421}$ **4.** $\frac{12}{29}$ **5.** $\cfrac{1}{7 + \cfrac{1}{6 + \cfrac{1}{5}}}$

6. $\cfrac{1}{10 + \cfrac{1}{5 + \frac{1}{2}}}$ **7.** $\cfrac{1}{2 + \cfrac{1}{3 + \cfrac{1}{4 + \frac{1}{5}}}}$ **8.** $\cfrac{1}{3 + \cfrac{1}{3 + \cfrac{1}{3 + \cfrac{1}{3 + \frac{1}{3}}}}}$

BONUS TOPIC 11
1. 9, 40, 41 **2.** 13, 84, 85
3.

p	q	$p^2 - q^2$	$2pq$	$p^2 + q^2$
2	1	3	4	5
3	2	5	12	13
4	1	15	8	17
4	3	7	24	25
5	2	21	20	29
5	4	9	40	41
6	1	35	12	37
6	5	11	60	61
7	2	45	28	53
7	4	33	56	65
7	6	13	84	85

4. Either a or b is divisible by 3; b is divisible by 4. **5.** Either
a, b, or c is divisible by 5 **6.** Either a, b, $a + b$, or $a - b$ is
divisible by 7.

BONUS TOPIC 12
1. 9 **2.** It is $\frac{1}{25}$ as bright. **3.** $27 million **4.** 6000

BONUS TOPIC 13

1. $y = x^2 + x + 1$ **2.** $y = 2x^2 - 2x - 1$
3. $y = x^2 + 3x - 4$ **4.** $y = 4x^2 - 5$

BONUS TOPIC 14

1. $a \approx 12.71$ **2.** $a \approx 11.06$ **3.** $a \approx 24.89$ **4.** $a \approx 4.13$

BONUS TOPIC 15

1. $\frac{1}{2}$ **2a.** $\frac{1}{2}$ **2b.** $\frac{1}{2}$ **3.** 0 **4.** $\frac{1}{8}$

CRITICAL THINKING 1

1a. **1b.** **1c.**

1d. **1e.** **2.**

3.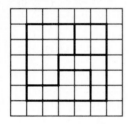

CRITICAL THINKING 2

1. C   **2.** B   **3.** D   **4.** E   **5.** E

CRITICAL THINKING 3

1. D   **2.** B   **3.** C   **4.** D   **5.** D   **6.** C

CRITICAL THINKING 4

CRITICAL THINKING 5

1. D (Jim)   **2.** B (Jill)   **3.** E (either Joe or Jill)
4. C (Jane)   **5.** E (Joe and Jane equally)
6. F (Joy and Jane equally)

CRITICAL THINKING 6

1. D   **2.** E   **3.** C   **4.** C

CRITICAL THINKING 7

1. $\frac{5}{13}$ **2.** $\frac{3}{8}$ **3.** $\frac{2}{5}$ **4.** The slopes are not equal.

Therefore, $\overline{AB}$ and $\overline{BC}$ do not lie on a straight line. There will be space, one square unit in area, between the two pieces 1 and 3 and the two pieces 2 and 4.

CRITICAL THINKING 8

1. D   **2.** A   **3.** D   **4.** B   **5.** D

CRITICAL THINKING 9

1.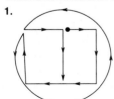

2.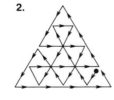

3.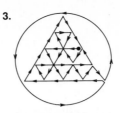

4.

CRITICAL THINKING 10

1. 33   **2.** 241   **3.** 113,010   **4.** 333,404   **5.** 70,307
6. 101,320

7.   **8.**

9.   **10.**

11.

12.

CRITICAL THINKING 11

1.

	1st	2nd	3rd	4th	5th	6th
Rosario	Music	Eng.	Sci.	Psych.	S.S.	Math
Lani	Eng.	Art	Hm.Ec.	Sci.	S.S.	Math
Erica	Eng.	Lang.	S.S.	Sci.	Auto	Math

2. Yes.

	1st	2nd	3rd	4th	5th	6th
Rosario	Music	Eng.	Art	Sci.	S.S.	Math
Lani	Eng.	Art	Hm.Ec.	Sci.	S.S.	Math
Erica	Math	Eng.	Art	Sci.	S.S.	Auto

3. No.

	1st	2nd	3rd	4th	5th	6th
Erica	Eng.	Lang.	S.S.	Sci.	Math	Auto

4. Erica's choice without rearrangement:

	1st	2nd	3rd	4th	5th	6th
Erica	Eng.	Art	S.S.	Sci.	Math	Auto

Erica's choices with rearrangement:

	1st	2nd	3rd	4th	5th	6th
Erica	Music	Eng.	S.S.	Sci.	Math	Auto
Erica	Music	Eng.	S.S.	Sci.	Auto	Math
Erica	Math	Eng.	Hm.Ec.	S.S.	Sci.	Auto
Erica	Eng.	Art	S.S.	Sci.	Auto	Math
Erica	Math	Eng.	Sci.	Psych.	S.S.	Auto

CRITICAL THINKING 12

1. C   **2.** B   **3.** C   **4.** B

CRITICAL THINKING 13

1. B   **2.** D   **3.** B

CRITICAL THINKING 14

1. D   **2.** B   **3.** A   **4.** D

CRITICAL THINKING 15

1. There are 15 possible pairs; 9 of them would show a 3. Thus, the probability of picking a 3 is 9 out of 15, $\frac{9}{15}$, or $\frac{3}{5}$.   **2.** The probability of not picking a 3 is $1 - \frac{3}{5}$, or $\frac{2}{5}$.   **3.** Since $\frac{3}{5} > \frac{2}{5}$ you are more likely to pick a 3.   **4.** The incorrect assumption is that there is a $\frac{1}{3}$ chance of getting a 5 with two number cubes. With two number cubes there are 36 possible outcomes. Out of the 36, these 11 combinations yield a 5: (5,1), (5,2), (5,3), (5,4), (5,5), (5,6), (6,5), (4,5), (3,5), (2,5), (1,5). You should not count (5,5) twice. Thus, the probability is $\frac{11}{36}$ and not $\frac{1}{3}$.

MANIPULATIVE ACTIVITY 1

1.

*	L	R	V	H
L	↓	↑	→	←
R	↑	↓	←	→
V	←	→	↑	↓
H	→	←	↓	↑

2a. ↑ **2b.** ↑ **2c.** ↓ **2d.** ↓
2e. → **2f.** ← **2g.** ↓ **2h.** ↓
3. No
4a. → **4b.** → **4c.** ↑ **4d.** ↓
4e. ↑ **4f.** ↑
5. No

MANIPULATIVE ACTIVITY 2

1a. No; there is a 1 in the 2's place. **1b.** No; there is a 1 in the 1's place. **1c.** 11 **2a.** 2 **2b.** 6 **2c.** 14 **3.** Put the paper clip through all holes in the 8's place and keep those cards that stay on the clip. **4.** Put the paper clip through all the holes in the 1's place and discard those that stay on the clip.

MANIPULATIVE ACTIVITY 3

1. 3 **2.** 2 **3.** 3 **4.** 7 **5.** 3 **6.** 3 **7.** 3 **8.** 4
9. 2 **10.** 6

MANIPULATIVE ACTIVITY 4

1. $A = 4$, $B = 3$, $C = 5$, $l = 4''$, $m = 4''$
2. $D = 3$, $E = 6$, $F = 4$, $x = 4''$, $y = 4''$

MANIPULATIVE ACTIVITY 5

1. 1225 **2.** 2025 **3.** 3025 **4.** 4225 **5.** 25
6. 2, 6, 12, 20, 30, and 42 **7.** The number of hundreds is equal to the product of the tens digit and the next greater digit.
8. $x + 1$ **9.** 5625 **10.** 7225 **11.** 9025 **12.** All

MANIPULATIVE ACTIVITY 6

1. $x^2 + 3x + 2$; $(x + 2)(x + 1)$ **2.** $x^2 - 7x + 10$; $(x - 5)(x - 2)$ **3.** $x^2 + 4x - 12$; $(x + 6)(x - 2)$

4. $(x + 5)(x + 3)$
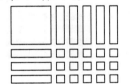

5. $(x - 3)^2$

6. $(x + 4)(x + 3)$

7. $(x - 5)(x - 3)$

8. $(x - 10)(x - 1)$

9. $(x + 8)(x + 1)$

10. $(x + 5)(x - 3)$
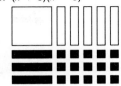

11. $(x + 2)(x - 9)$
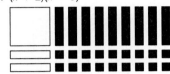

12. $(x + 2)(x - 8)$
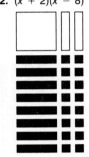

MANIPULATIVE ACTIVITY 7

1. Yes **2.** Positive **3–6.** Answers will vary.

MANIPULATIVE ACTIVITY 8

1. (2, 1) **2.** (−6, −2) **3.** (1, −3) **4.** (−2, 3)
5. (3, 5) **6.** (−3, −1) **7.** (−3, −5) The secret word is ALGEBRA.

MANIPULATIVE ACTIVITY 9

1. No **2.** No **3.** No **4.** Yes **5.** Yes **6.** Yes

MANIPULATIVE ACTIVITY 10

1. $x + 3$

2. $x - 2$

3. $x - 3$

4. $x - 5$
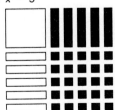

5. $x + 4 + \dfrac{-1}{x - 2}$

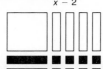

6. $x + 7 + \dfrac{5}{x - 2}$

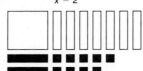

MANIPULATIVE ACTIVITY 11

No answers

MANIPULATIVE ACTIVITY 12

1. Answers will vary. **2.** Graphs will vary. **3.** Increasing
4. Increasing **5.** No **6.** No **7.** Nonlinear (curved)

MANIPULATIVE ACTIVITY 13

1. $x^2 + 10x + 25 = (x + 5)^2$

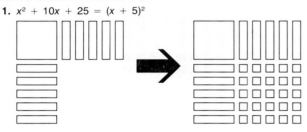

2. $x^2 - 8x + 16 = (x - 4)^2$

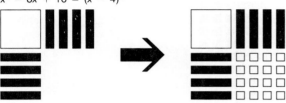

3. $x^2 - 18x + 81 = (x - 9)^2$

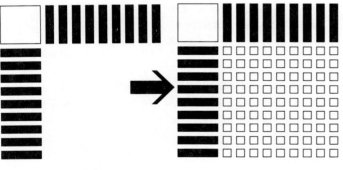

4. $x^2 + 7x + 12\frac{1}{4} = \left(x + 3\frac{1}{2}\right)^2$

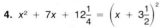
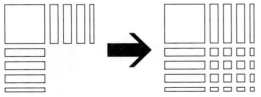

5. $\pm 12x$

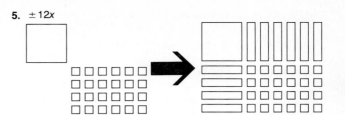

6. $\pm 16x$

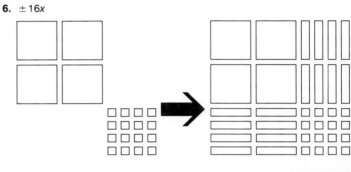

or

7. $\pm 6x$

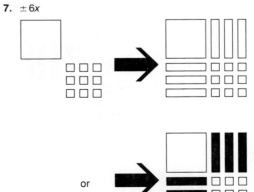

or

MANIPULATIVE ACTIVITY 14

△	a	b	c	sin A	∠A	cos B	∠B
1	1	1	$\sqrt{2}$	$\dfrac{\sqrt{2}}{2}$	45°	$\dfrac{\sqrt{2}}{2}$	45°
2	1	$\sqrt{2}$	$\sqrt{3}$	$\dfrac{\sqrt{3}}{3}$	35°	$\dfrac{\sqrt{3}}{3}$	55°
3	1	$\sqrt{3}$	2	$\dfrac{1}{2}$	30°	$\dfrac{1}{2}$	60°
4	1	2	$\sqrt{5}$	$\dfrac{\sqrt{5}}{5}$	26°	$\dfrac{\sqrt{5}}{5}$	54°

MANIPULATIVE ACTIVITY 15

1. $A = \pi r^2$ **2.** $2r \cdot 2r = 4r^2$ **3.** $\dfrac{\pi r^2}{4r^2} = \dfrac{\pi}{4}$ **4.** 0.785

6–8. Answers will vary.

LOOKING FOR ERRORS 1

1. ☐1 Incorrect operation
$x + 3$
$= 3 + x$

2. ☐1 Incorrect operation
$xy + 7$
$= 7 + xy$ (or $7 + yx$, or $yx + 7$)

3. ☐1 Incorrect operation
$4 + ab$
$= ab + 4$ (or $ba + 4$, or $4 + ba$)

4. ☐1 Incorrect operation
$\dfrac{5}{2} = \dfrac{5}{2} \cdot \dfrac{2}{2}$
$= \dfrac{10}{4}$

5. ☐1 Incorrect operation
$\dfrac{6}{9} = \dfrac{6}{9} \cdot \dfrac{4}{4}$
$= \dfrac{24}{36}$

6. No errors

7. ☐1 Incorrect operation
$(a + b) + c$
$= a + (b + c)$

8. ☐1 Incorrect operation
$(6 \cdot x) \cdot y$
$= 6 \cdot (x \cdot y)$

9. ☐1 Incorrect property
$4 \cdot (x \cdot y)$
$= (4 \cdot x) \cdot y$

10. ☐1 Incorrect application
$2(x + 3)$
$= 2 \cdot x + 2 \cdot 3$
$= 2x + 6$

11. ☐1 Incorrect application
$(x + y) \cdot 3$
$= x \cdot 3 + y \cdot 3$
$= 3x + 3y$

12. ☐1 Incorrect application
$9 \cdot (a + b)$
$= 9 \cdot a + 9 \cdot b$
$= 9a + 9b$

13. ☐1 Incorrect division
$7x + 14y$
$= 7 \cdot x + 7 \cdot 2y$
$= 7(x + 2y)$

14. ☐1 Incorrect application
$ax + bx$
$= a \cdot x + b \cdot x$
$= (a + b)x$

15. ☐2 Incorrect operation
$2x + 2y$
$= 2 \cdot x + 2 \cdot y$
$= 2(x + y)$

16. ☐2 Incorrect combining of terms
$6x + 4x^2 + 2x + 7$
$= 4x^2 + 6x + 2x + 7$
$= 4x^2 + (6 + 2)x + 7$
$= 4x^2 + 8x + 7$

17. ☐2 Incorrect factoring
$2x + y + 3x + y$
$= 2x + 3x + y + y$
$= (2 + 3)x + (1 + 1)y$
$= 5x + 2y$

18. ☐1 Incorrect operation
$a + b + 2a + b$
$= a + 2a + b + b$
$= (1 + 2)a + (1 + 1)b$
$= 3a + 2b$

LOOKING FOR ERRORS 2

1. ☐2 Incorrect sign
$-4(13)(-9)$
$= -4(-117)$
$= 468$

2. ☐1 Incorrect sign
$7(-3)(11)$
$= -21(11)$
$= -231$

3. ☐1 Incorrect sign
$-5(-2)(-12)$
$= 10(-12)$
$= -120$

4. ☐1 Incorrect sign
$\dfrac{4}{5}\left(-\dfrac{2}{3}\right)\left(-\dfrac{1}{2}\right)$
$= \dfrac{4}{5}\left(\dfrac{1}{3}\right)$
$= \dfrac{4}{15}$

5. ☐1 Incorrect sign
$\dfrac{3}{4}\left(-\dfrac{1}{4}\right)\left(\dfrac{1}{2}\right)$
$= -\dfrac{3}{16}\left(\dfrac{1}{2}\right)$
$= -\dfrac{3}{32}$

6. ☐1 Incorrect sign
$\dfrac{1}{7}(-3)(-6)$
$= \dfrac{1}{7}(18)$
$= \dfrac{18}{7}$

7. ☐1 Taking the reciprocal of the wrong term
$\dfrac{1}{8} \div \dfrac{1}{7}$
$= \dfrac{1}{8} \cdot \dfrac{7}{1}$
$= \dfrac{7}{8}$

8. ☐1 Incorrect operation
$\dfrac{2}{3} \div \dfrac{3}{4}$
$= \dfrac{2}{3} \cdot \dfrac{4}{3}$
$= \dfrac{8}{9}$

9. ☐1 Incorrect operation
$\dfrac{6}{7} \div \dfrac{1}{3}$
$= \dfrac{6}{7} \cdot \dfrac{3}{1}$
$= \dfrac{18}{7}$

10. ☐1 Did not use reciprocal
$\dfrac{1}{9} \div \dfrac{1}{4}$
$= \dfrac{1}{9} \cdot \dfrac{4}{1}$
$= \dfrac{4}{9}$

11. ☐1 Incorrect operation
$\dfrac{1}{3} \div \dfrac{2}{3}$
$= \dfrac{1}{3} \cdot \dfrac{3}{2}$
$= \dfrac{1}{2}$

12. ☐1 Taking reciprocal of wrong term
$\dfrac{2}{5} \div \dfrac{1}{4}$
$= \dfrac{2}{5} \cdot \dfrac{4}{1}$
$= \dfrac{8}{5}$

13. ☐1 Did not apply distributive property
$(-5)(3x) + (-5)(-3y)$
$+ (-5)(7)$
$-15x + 15y - 35$

14. No errors

15. ☐2 Incorrect factoring
$-\dfrac{1}{3}(a) + \left(-\dfrac{1}{3}\right)(-2b) + \left(-\dfrac{1}{3}\right)(3)$
$-\dfrac{1}{3}(a - 2b + 3)$

16. ☐2 Incomplete factoring
$x(y + z - 7)$

LOOKING FOR ERRORS 3

1. ☐1 Incorrect inverse operation
$3x = 12$
$3x \cdot \dfrac{1}{3} = 12 \cdot \dfrac{1}{3}$
$x = 4$

2. ☐1 Incorrect inverse operation
$a + 12 = 24$
$a + 12 - 12 = 24 - 12$
$a = 12$

3. ☐1 Incorrect reciprocal
$\dfrac{1}{4}z = 28$
$4 \cdot \dfrac{1}{4}z = 4 \cdot 28$
$z = 112$

4. ☐1 Adding 39 instead of subtracting
$3x + 39 = 69$
$3x + 39 - 39 = 69 - 39$
$3x = 30$
$\dfrac{1}{3} \cdot 3x = \dfrac{1}{3} \cdot 30$
$x = 10$

5. ☐3 Did not multiply by same number
$-7t + 36 = 71$
$-7t + 36 - 36 = 71 - 36$
$-7t = 35$
$-\dfrac{1}{7}(-7t) = -\dfrac{1}{7}(35)$
$t = -5$

6. ☐1 Did not factor correctly
$2x + 10x = 120$
$(2 + 10)x = 120$
$12x = 120$
$\dfrac{1}{12}(12x) = \dfrac{1}{12}(120)$
$x = 10$

7. No errors

8. ☐1 Did not use   OR   ☐1 Did not
distributive property   subtract first

$4 + \frac{1}{2}m = 20$ $4 + \frac{1}{2}m = 20$

$2\left(4 + \frac{1}{2}m\right) = 2(20)$ $4 + \frac{1}{2}m - 4 = 20 - 4$

$8 + m = 40$ $\frac{1}{2}m = 16$
$8 + m - 8 = 40 - 8$
$m = 32$ $2\left(\frac{1}{2}m\right) = 2(16)$

                                      $m = 32$

9. ☐1 Used incorrect additive inverse   **10.** No errors
$-5 + 2x = 17$
$-5 + 2x + 5 = 17 + 5$
$2x = 22$
$\frac{1}{2}(2x) = \frac{1}{2}(22)$
$x = 11$

11. ☐1 Incorrect combining of   **12.** ☐1 Did not use
like terms   distributive property
$6y - 5 + 5y + 35 = y$ $5x = 10x + 50$
$(6 + 5)y + (-5 + 35) = y$ $5x \cdot \frac{1}{5} = (10x + 50) \cdot \frac{1}{5}$
$11y + 30 = y$
$11y + 30 - y = y - y$ $x = \frac{1}{5}(10x) + \frac{1}{5}(50)$
$10y + 30 = 0$
$10y + 30 - 30 = 0 - 30$ $x = 2x + 10$
$10y = -30$ $x - 2x = 2x + 10 - 2x$
$\frac{1}{10}(10y) = \frac{1}{10}(-30)$ $-x = 10$
                                      $(-1)(-x) = (-1)(10)$
$y = -3$ $x = -10$

13. ☐1 Incorrect reciprocal   **14.** ☐1 Incorrect inverse
$\frac{3}{wl} \cdot V = \frac{3}{wl} \cdot \frac{1}{3} wlh$ operation
                                      $r \cdot F = r \cdot \frac{mv^2}{r}$
$\frac{3V}{wl} = h$ $rF = mv^2$
                                      $rF \cdot \frac{1}{F} = mv^2 \cdot \frac{1}{F}$
                                      $r = \frac{mv^2}{F}$

LOOKING FOR ERRORS 4

1. No errors   **2.** ☐3 Incorrect graph

3. ☐2 Adding instead of subtracting 4   **4.** No errors
$2y + 4 - y > 6$
$y + 4 > 6$
$y + 4 - 4 > 6 - 4$
$y > 2$

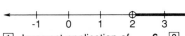

5. ☐1 Incorrect application of   **6.** ☐2 Incorrect change of
multiplication rules   inequality sign
$-5y \le 25$ $16x > -64$
$\left(-\frac{1}{5}\right)(-5y) \ge \left(-\frac{1}{5}\right)(25)$ $\frac{1}{16}(16x) > \frac{1}{16}(-64)$
$y \ge -5$ $x > -4$

7. ☐2 Incorrect multiplication   **8.** No errors
$-55 \ge -11x$
$\left(-\frac{1}{11}\right)(-55) \le \left(-\frac{1}{11}\right)(-11x)$
$5 \le x$

9. At most also includes   **10.** Incorrect inequality sign
equal to $30n < 30$
$2x \le 40$
11. No errors   **12.** No errors
13. Incorrect coefficient for   **14.** No errors
variable
$3y < 9$

LOOKING FOR ERRORS 5

1. ☐2 Incorrect application of rules of   **2.** No errors
exponents
$(x^5)^2$
$= x^5 \cdot x^5$
$= x^{5+5}$
$= x^{10}$

3. ☐4 Incorrect addition of terms
$(x^3 + 6x^2 + x) - (x^3 - 2x^2)$
$= (x^3 + 6x^2 + x) + (-x^3 + 2x^2)$
$\quad\quad x^3 + 6x^2 + x$
$\underline{+ (-x^3 + 2x^2 + 0)}$
$\quad\quad\quad 8x^2 + x$

4. ☐1 Failure to change all signs
$(5x^2 + 7x + 2) - (x^2 - 3)$
$= (5x^2 + 7x + 2) + (-x^2 + 3)$
$\quad\quad 5x^2 + 7x + 2$
$\underline{+ (-x^2 + 0x + 3)}$
$\quad\quad 4x^2 + 7x + 5$

5. ☐1 Incorrect sign
$(x + 2)(x - 2)$
$= x(x - 2) + 2(x - 2)$
$= x^2 - 2x + 2x - 4$
$= x^2 - 4$

6. ☐4 Incorrect combining of like terms
$(x + 7)^2$
$= (x + 7)(x + 7)$
$= x(x + 7) + 7(x + 7)$
$= x^2 + 7x + 7x + 49$
$= x^2 + 14x + 49$

7. ☐2 Incorrect application of distributive property
$(2x - 3)^2$
$= (2x - 3)(2x - 3)$
$= 2x(2x - 3) - 3(2x - 3)$
$= 4x^2 - 6x - 6x + 9$
$= 4x^2 - 12x + 9$

8. No errors
9. ☐1 Incorrect application of distributive property
$(x - 2)(x^3 + 7x + 2)$
$= x(x^3 + 7x + 2) - 2(x^3 + 7x + 2)$
$= x^4 + 7x^2 + 2x - 2x^3 - 14x - 4$
$= x^4 - 2x^3 + 7x^2 - 12x - 4$

10. No errors   **11.** ☐2 Incorrect multiplication of integers
$(x - 3)(x^4 + 3x - 7)$
$= x(x^4 + 3x - 7) - 3(x^4 + 3x - 7)$
$= x^5 + 3x^2 - 7x - 3x^4 - 9x + 21$
$= x^5 - 3x^4 + 3x^2 - 16x + 21$

LOOKING FOR ERRORS 6

1. ☐2 Incorrect division   **2.** ☐1 Incomplete factoring
$9x^2 + 9$ $7x^2 - 21x$
$= 9(x^2 + 1)$ $= 7x(x) - 7x(3)$
                                      $= 7x(x - 3)$

3. ☐1 Incomplete factoring   **4.** ☐1 Incomplete factoring
$60a^2b - 40a^2$ $2x^2 + 10x + 12$
$= 20a^2(3b) - 20a^2(2)$ $= 2(x^2 + 5x + 6)$
$= 20a^2(3b - 2)$ $= 2(x + 3)(x + 2)$

5. ☐1 Incomplete factoring   **6.** No errors.
$4x^2 - 4x - 48$
$= 4(x^2 - x - 12)$
$= 4(x - 4)(x + 3)$

7. ☐1 Incomplete factoring   **8.** ☐1 Incomplete factoring
$2x^2 + 4x - 48$ $7x^2 - 14x - 21$
$= 2(x^2 + 2x - 24)$ $= 7(x^2 - 2x - 3)$
$= 2(x + 6)(x - 4)$ $= 7(x - 3)(x + 1)$

9. ☐1 Incomplete factoring   **10.** ☐2 Incomplete factoring
$6x^2 + 30x + 36$ $2x^3 - 2x^2 + 6x - 6$
$= 6(x^2 + 5x + 6)$ $= 2(x^3 - x^2 + 3x - 3)$
$= 6(x + 3)(x + 2)$ $= 2(x^2(x - 1) + 3(x - 1))$
                                      $= 2(x^2 + 3)(x - 1)$

11. ☐2 Incomplete factoring
$3x^3 + 3x^2 + 9x + 9$
$= 3(x^3 + x^2 + 3x + 3)$
$= 3(x^2(x + 1) + 3(x + 1))$
$= 3(x^2 + 3)(x + 1)$

12. ☐2 Incomplete factoring
$x^3 + 4x^2 - x - 4$
$= x^2(x + 4) - 1(x + 4)$
$= (x^2 - 1)(x + 4)$
$= (x - 1)(x + 1)(x + 4)$

13. ☐2 Incomplete factoring
$2x^3 + 6x^2 + 4x$
$= 2x(x^2 + 3x + 2)$
$= 2x(x + 2)(x + 1)$

14. ☐1 Incomplete factoring
$3x^2 + 3x - 6$
$= 3(x^2 + x - 2)$
$= 3(x + 2)(x - 1)$

15. ☐2 Incomplete factoring
$4x^2 - 20x + 24$
$= 4(x^2 - 5x + 6)$
$= 4(x - 3)(x - 2)$

16. ☐1 Incorrect factoring
$-3x^2 + 12y^2$
$= -3(x^2 - 4y^2)$
$= -3(x - 2y)(x + 2y)$

17. ☐1 Cannot be factored.

18. ☐1 Incorrect factoring
$4p^2 - 9q^2$
$= (2p - 3q)(2p + 3q)$

LOOKING FOR ERRORS 7

1. ☐1 Incorrect substitution
$\dfrac{5 - (-2)}{3 - 2}$
$= \dfrac{7}{1}$
$= 7$
The slope is 7.

2. ☐1 Incorrect substitution
$\dfrac{3 - (-3)}{3 - (-3)}$
$= \dfrac{6}{6}$
$= 1$
The slope is 1.

3. No errors

4. ☐2 Incorrect form
$2x - y = 4$
$-y = 4 - 2x$
$y = 2x - 4$
The slope is 2.

5. ☐1 Incorrect operation
$4y = 3x$
$y = \dfrac{3}{4}x$
The slope is $\dfrac{3}{4}$.

6. ☐2 Incorrect form
$2x - 6y = 37$
$-6y = -2x + 37$
$6y = 2x - 37$
$y = \dfrac{1}{3}x - \dfrac{37}{6}$
The slope is $\dfrac{1}{3}$.

7. ☐1 Incorrect sign
$4y + x = 9$
$4y = -x + 9$
$y = -\dfrac{1}{4}x + \dfrac{9}{4}$
The slope is $-\dfrac{1}{4}$.

8. ☐2 Incorrect coefficient
$y - x = 13$
$y = x + 13$
The slope is 1.

9. ☐3 Incorrect coefficient
$6x + 2y = 10$
$2y = 10 - 6x$
$y = 5 - 3x$
The slope is -3.

10. ☐1 Incorrect form
$y = 3x + 2$

11. Incorrect form
$y = \dfrac{1}{3}x + 1$

12. Incorrect form
$y = 0$

LOOKING FOR ERRORS 8

1. ☐1 Incorrect substitution
$x + y = 6$
$x = 4 + y$
Substitute $4 + y$ for x.
$(4 + y) + y = 6$
$4 + 2y = 6$
$2y = 2$
$y = 1$
Substitute 1 for y.
$x = 4 + 1$
$x = 5$
The answer is (5, 1).

2. ☐2 Incorrect subtraction
$2y - x = 3$
$x = y + 7$
Substitute $y + 7$ for x.
$2y - (y + 7) = 3$
$2y - y - 7 = 3$
$y - 7 = 3$
$y = 10$
Substitute 10 for y.
$x = 10 + 7$
$x = 17$
The answer is (17, 10).

3. ☐2 Incorrect multiplication
$y + 2x = 9$
$x = y - 3$
Substitute $y - 3$ for x.
$y + 2(y - 3) = 9$
$y + 2y - 6 = 9$
$3y - 6 = 9$
$3y = 15$
$y = 5$
Substitute 5 for y.
$x = 5 - 3$
$x = 2$
The answer is (2, 5).

4. ☐1 Incorrect addition
$\begin{array}{r} x + y = 12 \\ x - y = 4 \\ \hline 2x = 16 \\ x = 8 \end{array}$
The answer is (8, 4).

5. ☐1 Incorrect addition
$\begin{array}{r} -x + y = 6 \\ x + y = 2 \\ \hline 2y = 8 \\ y = 4 \end{array}$
The answer is $(-2, 4)$.

6. No errors

7. ☐1 Incorrect addition
$\begin{array}{r} y - x = 10 \\ -y - x = 2 \\ \hline -2x = 12 \\ x = -6 \end{array}$
The answer is $(-6, 4)$.

8. No errors

9. ☐1 Incorrect addition
$\begin{array}{r} x + y = 16 \\ x - y = 2 \\ \hline 2x = 18 \\ x = 9 \end{array}$
The answer is (9, 7).

LOOKING FOR ERRORS 9

1. ☐3 Incorrect graph
$2 < x + 3 \le 3$
$2 < x + 3$ and $x + 3 \le 3$
$-1 < x$ and $x \le 0$

2. No errors

3. ☐2 Incorrect graph
$2x < 4$ or $x + 3 < 7$
$x < 2$ or $x < 4$
$x < 4$

4. No errors

5. No errors

6. ☐1 Incorrect interpretation of absolute value
$\left| \dfrac{1}{3}x - 2 \right| = 6$
$\dfrac{1}{3}x - 2 = 6$ or $\dfrac{1}{3}x - 2 = -6$
$\dfrac{1}{3}x = 8$ or $\dfrac{1}{3}x = -4$
$x = 24$ or $x = -12$

7. No errors

8. ☐1 Incomplete consideration of absolute value
$|9x - 4| = 14$
$9x - 4 = 14$ or $9x - 4 = -14$
$9x = 18$ or $9x = -10$
$x = 2$ or $x = -\dfrac{10}{9}$

9. ☐3 Incorrect conclusion
Test the point (0, 0)
$0 - 0 = 0$
But $0 \not< 0$
No

10. ☐1 Incorrect substitution
Test the point $\left(\dfrac{1}{2}, -\dfrac{1}{4} \right)$
$7\left(-\dfrac{1}{4} \right) + 9\left(\dfrac{1}{2} \right) = \dfrac{11}{4}$
$\dfrac{11}{4} > -3$
Yes

LOOKING FOR ERRORS 10

1. ☒ Incorrect split of rational expression

$$\frac{x^2 + 2x + 1}{x^2 - 1}$$
$$= \frac{(x + 1)(x + 1)}{(x + 1)(x - 1)}$$
$$= \frac{x + 1}{x - 1}$$

2. ☒ Incorrect division procedure

$$\frac{x^2 + 7x + 12}{x + 3}$$
$$= \frac{(x + 3)(x + 4)}{x + 3}$$
$$= x + 4$$

3. No errors

4. ☐ Incorrect common denominator

$$\frac{7a}{b} + \frac{4a}{b}$$
$$= \frac{7a + 4a}{b}$$
$$= \frac{11a}{b}$$

5. ☒ Incorrect combining of like terms

$$\frac{3x}{y} + \frac{7}{y}$$
$$= \frac{3x + 7}{y}$$

6. ☒ Incorrect combining of like terms

$$\frac{4x}{6} + \frac{3x}{6}$$
$$= \frac{4x + 3x}{6}$$
$$= \frac{7x}{6}$$

7. ☒ Incorrect product

$$\frac{6}{a} + \frac{a}{a^2}$$
$$= \frac{6}{a} \cdot \frac{a}{a} + \frac{a}{a^2}$$
$$= \frac{6a}{a^2} + \frac{a}{a^2}$$
$$= \frac{6a + a}{a^2}$$
$$= \frac{7a}{a^2}$$
$$= \frac{7}{a}$$

8. No errors **9.** No errors

10. No errors

11. ☒ Incorrect subtraction

$$\begin{array}{r} x + 3 \\ x - 2 \overline{)x^2 + x - 6} \\ \underline{x^2 - 2x} \\ 3x - 6 \\ \underline{3x - 6} \\ 0 \end{array}$$

LOOKING FOR ERRORS 11

1. ☐ Incorrect application of rule

$$\sqrt{7} \cdot \sqrt{x}$$
$$= \sqrt{7x}$$

2. No errors

3. ☒ Incorrect multiplication

$$\sqrt{\frac{1}{2}} \cdot \sqrt{\frac{3}{2}}$$
$$= \sqrt{\frac{1}{2} \cdot \frac{3}{2}}$$
$$= \sqrt{\frac{3}{4}} = \frac{\sqrt{3}}{2}$$

4. ☐ Incorrect multiplication

$$\sqrt{2} \cdot \sqrt{x + 1}$$
$$= \sqrt{2(x + 1)}$$
$$= \sqrt{2x + 2}$$

5. ☒ Incorrect equivalence

$$\frac{\sqrt{3}}{\sqrt{9}}$$
$$= \frac{\sqrt{3}}{3}$$
$$= \frac{1}{3}\sqrt{3}$$

6. ③ Incorrect square root

$$\frac{\sqrt{20x^2}}{\sqrt{10}}$$
$$= \sqrt{\frac{20x^2}{10}}$$
$$= \sqrt{2x^2}$$
$$= x\sqrt{2}$$

7. No errors **8.** ☒ Incorrect multiplication

$$\frac{\sqrt{5}}{\sqrt{3}}$$
$$= \frac{\sqrt{5}}{\sqrt{3}} \cdot \frac{\sqrt{3}}{\sqrt{3}}$$
$$= \frac{\sqrt{15}}{3}$$
$$= \frac{1}{3}\sqrt{15}$$

9. ☐ Incorrect factoring

$$2\sqrt{3} + 5\sqrt{3}$$
$$= (2 + 5)\sqrt{3}$$
$$= 7\sqrt{3}$$

10. ☐ Incorrect addition

$$\sqrt{5} + \sqrt{20}$$
$$= \sqrt{5} + 2\sqrt{5}$$
$$= (1 + 2)\sqrt{5}$$
$$= 3\sqrt{5}$$

11. ☐ Incorrect subtraction

$$\sqrt{16x - 16} - \sqrt{9x - 9}$$
$$= \sqrt{16(x - 1)} - \sqrt{9(x - 1)}$$
$$= 4\sqrt{x - 1} - 3\sqrt{x - 1}$$
$$= (4 - 3)\sqrt{x - 1}$$
$$= \sqrt{x - 1}$$

12. ☐ Incorrect factoring

$$16\sqrt{y} - \sqrt{y}$$
$$= (16 - 1)\sqrt{y}$$
$$= 15\sqrt{y}$$

13. ☐ Incorrect relationship among sides

$$2^2 + b^2 = 5^2$$
$$4 + b^2 = 25$$
$$b^2 = 25 - 4$$
$$b^2 = 21$$
$$b = \sqrt{21}$$

14. No errors

15. ☐ Incorrect relationship among sides

$$a^2 + 2^2 = 6^2$$
$$a^2 + 4 = 36$$
$$a^2 = 36 - 4$$
$$a^2 = 32$$
$$a = \sqrt{32}, \text{ or } 4\sqrt{2}$$

LOOKING FOR ERRORS 12

1. Incorrect substitution in all

$$h(2) = 7(2) - 12 \quad h(9) = 7(9) - 12$$
$$= 14 - 12 \qquad\quad = 63 - 12$$
$$= 2 \qquad\qquad\quad = 51$$
$$h(16) = 7(16) - 12 \quad h(23) = 7(23) - 12$$
$$= 112 - 12 \qquad\quad = 161 - 12$$
$$= 100 \qquad\qquad\quad = 149$$

2. Incorrect identification of linear function; graph must be a line

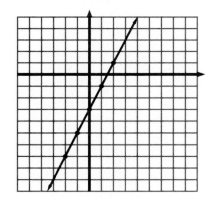

3. ⑥ Incorrect substitution

$$B = \frac{0.17}{3}$$
$$\approx 0.0567$$

The light's brightness from 3 miles would be approximately 0.0567.

LOOKING FOR ERRORS 13

1. [1] Failed to obtain 0 on one side of equation

$x^2 + x = 6$

$x^2 + x - 6 = 0$

$(x + 3)(x - 2) = 0$

$x + 3 = 0$ or $x - 2 = 0$

$x = -3$ or 2

2. No errors

3. [2] Solved equation incorrectly

$x^2 + 2x - 8 = 0$

$(x + 4)(x - 2) = 0$

$x + 4 = 0$ or $x - 2 = 0$

$x = -4$ or 2

4. [1] Did not attempt to find second root

$(x + 6)^2 = 16$

$x + 6 = \pm\sqrt{16}$

$x + 6 = \pm 4$

$x = -6 \pm 4$

$x = -2$ or -10

5. No errors

6. [1] Incorrect operation

$-5x^2 - 1 = -1$

$-5x^2 = 0$

$x^2 = 0$

$x = 0$

7. [4] Did not attempt to find second root

$x^2 + 6x - 4 = 0$

$x^2 + 6x = 4$

$x^2 + 6x + 9 = 4 + 9$

$(x + 3)^2 = 13$

$x + 3 = \pm\sqrt{13}$

$x = -3 \pm\sqrt{13}$

$x = -3 + \sqrt{13}$ or $-3 - \sqrt{13}$

8. [2] Incorrect number used to complete the square

$x^2 - 8x + 1 = 0$

$x^2 - 8x = -1$

$x^2 - 8x + 16 = -1 + 16$

$(x - 4)^2 = 15$

$x - 4 = \pm\sqrt{15}$

$x = 4 \pm\sqrt{15}$

$x = 4 + \sqrt{15}$ or $4 - \sqrt{15}$

9. No errors

10. [7] Did not check possible roots

check: $\sqrt{19 - 6x} + 5 = x + 3$

$\sqrt{19 - 6(-5)} + 5 = -5 + 3$

$\sqrt{19 + 30} + 5 = -2$

$\sqrt{49} + 5 = -2$

$7 + 5 = -2$

$12 \neq -2$

check: $\sqrt{19 - 6x} + 5 = x + 3$

$\sqrt{19 - 6(3)} + 5 = 3 + 3$

$\sqrt{19 - 18} + 5 = 6$

$\sqrt{1} + 5 = 6$

$1 + 5 = 6$

$6 = 6$

$x = 3$ is the only solution.

LOOKING FOR ERRORS 14

1. [1] Incorrect proportion

$\dfrac{12}{6} = \dfrac{a}{3\sqrt{5}}$

$3\sqrt{5}\left(\dfrac{12}{6}\right) = \dfrac{a}{3\sqrt{5}}(3\sqrt{5})$

$\dfrac{12\sqrt{5}}{2} = a$

$a = 6\sqrt{5}$

2. [1] Incorrect proportion

$\dfrac{b}{4\sqrt{2}} = \dfrac{6}{8}$

$4\sqrt{2}\left(\dfrac{b}{4\sqrt{2}}\right) = \dfrac{6}{8}(4\sqrt{2})$

$b = \dfrac{6\sqrt{2}}{2}$

$b = 3\sqrt{2}$

3. No errors

4. [1] Incorrect proportion

$\dfrac{5}{10} = \dfrac{a}{\sqrt{89}}$

$\sqrt{89}\left(\dfrac{5}{10}\right) = \dfrac{a}{\sqrt{89}}(\sqrt{89})$

$\dfrac{5\sqrt{89}}{10} = a$

$a = \dfrac{\sqrt{89}}{2}$

5. [1] Incorrect proportion

$\dfrac{8}{10} = \dfrac{b}{5\sqrt{2}}$

$5\sqrt{2}\left(\dfrac{8}{10}\right) = \dfrac{b}{5\sqrt{2}}(5\sqrt{2})$

$\dfrac{8\sqrt{2}}{2} = b$

$b = 4\sqrt{2}$

6. [1] Incorrect proportion

$\dfrac{b}{2\sqrt{29}} = \dfrac{7}{14}$

$2\sqrt{29}\left(\dfrac{b}{2\sqrt{29}}\right) = \dfrac{7}{14}(2\sqrt{29})$

$b = \dfrac{14\sqrt{29}}{14}$

$b = \sqrt{29}$

LOOKING FOR ERRORS 15

1. [2] Incorrect probability for each event

$P(\text{even}) = P(2) + P(4) + P(6)$

$= \dfrac{1}{6} + \dfrac{1}{6} + \dfrac{1}{6}$

$= \dfrac{3}{6}$, or $\dfrac{1}{2}$

2. [1] Cannot count the same event twice

$P(<4) + P(\text{odd}) - P(<4 \cap \text{odd})$

$= (P(1) + P(2) + P(3) + P(1) + P(3) + P(5) + P(7) + P(9)) - (P(1) + P(3))$

$= \left(\dfrac{1}{10} + \dfrac{1}{10} + \dfrac{1}{10} + \dfrac{1}{10} + \dfrac{1}{10} + \dfrac{1}{10} + \dfrac{1}{10} + \dfrac{1}{10}\right) - \left(\dfrac{1}{10} + \dfrac{1}{10}\right)$

$= \dfrac{8}{10} - \dfrac{2}{10}$

$= \dfrac{6}{10}$, or $\dfrac{3}{5}$

3. Labels on the horizontal and vertical axes are transposed.

4. [1] [2] [3] Terms are mixed up

Mean: $\dfrac{64}{11}$, or $5\dfrac{9}{11}$

Median: 6

Mode: 7

PROBABILITY/STATISTICS 1

Answers will vary depending upon experiment and data collected.

PROBABILITY/STATISTICS 2

1–5. Answers will vary.

6.

		Numbers on Die 1					
		1	2	3	4	5	6
	1	2	3	4	5	6	7
Numbers	2	3	4	5	6	7	8
on Die 2	3	4	5	6	7	8	9
	4	5	6	7	8	9	10
	5	6	7	8	9	10	11
	6	7	8	9	10	11	12

$P(\text{odd sum}) = \dfrac{18}{36}$, or $\dfrac{1}{2}$.

$P(\text{even sum}) = \dfrac{18}{36}$, or $\dfrac{1}{2}$.

7. Yes   **8.** Answers will vary.

PROBABILITY/STATISTICS 3

1–6. Answers will depend upon class data.

EXTRA: James Polk (1796) and Warren Harding (1865) were born on November 2. John Adams (1826), Thomas Jefferson (1826), and James Monroe (1831) all died on July 4.

PROBABILITY/STATISTICS 4

1–5. Answers will depend upon class data.

6. $P(0) = \frac{1}{36}$, $P(1) = \frac{2}{36}$, $P(2) = \frac{3}{36}$, $P(3) = \frac{3}{36}$, $P(4) = \frac{4}{36}$, $P(5) = \frac{5}{36}$, $P(6) = \frac{5}{36}$, $P(7) = \frac{4}{36}$, $P(8) = \frac{3}{36}$, $P(9) = \frac{3}{36}$, $P(10) = \frac{2}{36}$, $P(11) = \frac{1}{36}$

PROBABILITY/STATISTICS 5

1.

Stem	Leaf
5	8
6	0 2 3 3
7	0 4 4 4 5 5 5 6 6 7 7 7 8 8 8 8 8 9 9
8	0 0 0 0 1 1 2 2 3 4 5 5 6 6 6 7 7 7 8 8 8 8 9 9 9 9 9
9	0 1 6
10	2 7

2. Answers will vary.

3. Mean = 81.05; median = 80.5; mode = 78 and 89 (bimodal) No city has the mean, although Columbus and Seattle are close. No city has the median, although Albany, Pittsburgh, St. Louis, and Salt Lake City lie just below, and Columbus and Seattle lie just above. The data is bimodal: Denver, Detroit, Spokane, Topeka, and Tulsa all have 78; Albuquerque, Portland, Raleigh, Richmond, and San Antonio all have 89.

4–6. Answers depend upon class data.

PROBABILITY/STATISTICS 6

1. Let a, b, c, d, and e represent the numbers.
Then $0 \le a \le b \le c \le d \le e$.
The median is 5; so $0 \le a \le b \le 5 \le d \le e$.
The mode is 7; so $0 \le a \le b \le 5 \le 7 \le 7$.
The mean is 5; so $a + b + 19 = 25$, or $a + b = 6$. The only pair of numbers for a and b that satisfy all conditions is 2 and 4. So, the solution is $\{2, 4, 5, 7, 7\}$.

2. All should have found the same set. **3.** One
4. a. 0 **b.** 1 **c.** 0 **d.** 0 **e.** 0
5. Several solutions are possible, including $\{5, 5, 5, 5, 5\}$, $\{4, 5, 5, 5, 6\}$, $\{3, 5, 5, 5, 7\}$, etc.
6. Conditions: $0 \le a \le b \le c \le d \le e \le 20$, and $2a + d + e < 4c$. Several solutions are possible, including $\{0, 0, 0, 20, 20\}$.
7. Conditions: $a + b + c + d + e < 5c$, and $a + b + c + d + e < $ mode. One possible solution is $\{0, 0, 5, 5, 5\}$.
8. If the mode is less than the median, then $\{a, a, b, c, d\}$. If the mean is less than the mode, then $2a + b + c + d < 5a$, or $b + c + d < 3a$. But $b > a$, $c > a$, and $d > a$ in order to satisfy the first condition. So, $b + c + d > 3a$. The contradiction reveals that there is no solution.
9. At least two examples are $\{0, 0, 0, 20, 20\}$ and $\{0, 0, 20, 20, 20\}$.

PROBABILITY/STATISTICS 7

1–6. Answers depend upon class data.
EXTRA 7. They must score at least 12 runs during the 3 games. One way to find the different ways in which this can be done is to make a chart.

Game 1	Game 2	Game 3
12	0	0
0	12	0
0	0	12
11	1	0
11	0	1
1	11	0
	etc.	

There are 91 ways in all in which the additional 12 runs may be scored.